MEET
JESUS

MEET JESUS

ROBERT BADENAS

About the author . . .

For twenty-five years Dr. Robert Badenas has studied and taught New Testament in colleges and universities in both Europe and the USA. Spanish by birth, Dr. Badenas is at present Professor of New Testament at Collonges-sous-Saleve Theological Seminary in France.

In its Spanish, Portuguese, French and Italian editions MEET JESUS has already sold widely in Europe and Latin America. MEET JESUS has played a vital role in the revival now sweeping Central and South America. Its deep spiritual insights and compelling, readable style have brought tens of thousands to the foot of Calvary's cross.

This is the first English edition of this powerful book. . . .

Translator
ANNETTE DUNBEBIN-MELGOSA

Copyright © 1995 by Robert Badenas
First published in English edition 1995
All rights reserved. No part of this publication may be reproduced in any form without prior permission from the publisher.
ISBN 1-873796-47-1

Printed and published by
Autumn House,
Alma Park, Grantham, Lincolnshire,
NG31 9SL, England

Contents

Introduction	7
In the desert	9
In the night	20
By the well	29
At the beach	35
In the courtyard	43
At the foot of the mountain	49
At dawn	59
On a trip	69
At home	78
Along the way	84
Under a tree	92
At the feast	99
At a supper	107
Under the columns	113
In the evening	127
Among friends	133

List of Abbreviations

To reduce the section of Notes, sources used have been abbreviated as follows:

Abbreviations of Biblical Books

Gen.	Genesis	Matt.	Matthew
Exod.	Exodus	Mark	Mark
Lev.	Leviticus	Luke	Luke
Num.	Numbers	John	John
Deut.	Deuteronomy	Acts	Acts
Jos.	Joshua	Rom.	Romans
Judg.	Judges	1 Cor.	1 Corinthians
2 Sam.	2 Samuel	2 Cor.	2 Corinthians
1 Kgs	1 Kings	Gal.	Galatians
2 Kgs	2 Kings	Eph.	Ephesians
2 Chr.	2 Chronicles	Phil.	Philippians
Ezra	Ezra	Col.	Colossians
Neh.	Nehemiah	1 Thess.	1 Thessalonians
Job	Job	1 Tim.	1 Timothy
Ps.	Psalms	Titus	Titus
Prov.	Proverbs	Heb.	Hebrews
Isa.	Isaiah	1 Peter	1 Peter
Jer.	Jeremiah	1 John	1 John
Ezek.	Ezekiel	2 John	2 John
Dan.	Daniel	Rev.	Revelation
Hos.	Hosea		
Obad.	Obadiah		
Mic.	Micah		
Zech.	Zechariah		
Mal.	Malachi		

Abbreviations of the works of Flavius Josephus

Ant.	Jewish Antiquities
War	The Jewish War
Life	The Life

Abbreviations of Rabbinical Writings

The Babylonian Talmud is indicated by a 'b' before the title. The Jerusalem Talmud is indicated by a 'j'.

The transliteration of the names of the rabbinical writings is based on *The Mishnah* (H. Danby, ed.) Oxford: University Press, 1977.

Introduction

Though examined and re-examined by the greatest minds, some literary works can never fully be understood or appreciated. The human heart revels in their matchless value and literary genius, and the passing years only increase their beauty and timelessness.

Among such proven treasures we find the four gospels which tell the story of the most complex and unique Figure in all history. These eloquent pages, however, mark only the threshold of a vast collection of works about Jesus.[1]

The number of books about this exceptional Being, who reaches beyond the schemes of humanity, makes one wonder if anything more needs to be said. However, I do not choose to write these pages for lack of published material. Rather, the inexhaustible attraction of Jesus encourages me to add my contribution.

Just as we can appreciate sublime symphonies, majestic cathedrals, and other outstanding works of art from different perspectives, so the gospels can be appreciated from different viewpoints. I do not pretend to follow a biographical or theological approach to the life of Christ. The many great works already in existence need no amplification. Instead, I have chosen the story-telling approach. The gospel stories were originally written down so that future generations could relive them again and again, and thus be led to the Saviour.[2] It is my hope that, through this work, the gospels will continue to speak to each one of us.

Instead of using the biblical text in all its sacred and inflexible authority, I have chosen to draw upon its vitality through its unlimited flexibility and relevance. Faithfulness to the intention of the text permits me such liberty. I presume to tell of these encounters in my own way because I know that, before being recorded, they were related by witnesses.

Through twenty-five years of teaching, I have accumulated many documents (see notes at the end of each chapter).

In the hope of closing the cultural and historical gap, I try to present a picture of the true surroundings and personalities in each story. Clarity is my foremost concern. I use archaeological facts when such use makes the underlying truth of each story more evident.

However, in this work I avoid the purely historical account and theological analysis of the chosen biblical passages as ends in themselves. Rather, I choose to help the reader 'live' certain scenes from the life of Jesus so he or she can 'feel' their relevance as they touch Him.

If this brief work ignites within you a spark of interest in exploring the gospels in more details, or if it helps you to find or refind Jesus, it will have obtained its objective.

I must thank Annette Dunbebin-Melgosa for her enthusiastic and tireless work in the translation and preparation of the English manuscript.

---

[1] John 21:25.
[2] 2 Cor. 3:4-6.

In the desert

The Jordan river snakes its way down through the desert, dropping nearly 1,300 feet below sea level before finally entering the stagnant waters of the Dead Sea. The lowest area on earth, this is a place steeped in history.[1]

It seems hard to believe that this desert land, so tortured by erosion and scorched by the fire of heaven, once embraced the city of Sodom in its fertile valley.[2] Not even Jericho's dark-green oasis of palm trees can soften the feeling of desolation as one looks upon these broken heaps of stones and lifeless ruins.[3]

The sound of early-morning travellers splashing through the waters of Bethabara[4] rudely echoes from sharp peaks and black crevices, and awakens the sleeping hills. All caravans must cross the river at this point. Here Joshua led the Israelites across the Jordan on dry ground into the Promised Land.[5] This also marks the spot where Elijah opened the turbulent waters with his mantle and where, later, he ascended to heaven in a chariot of fire.[6]

Here the river flows slowly as it rounds a large bend and finally comes to rest in a quiet pool. Released from the tortuous river bed at last, the water laps a sandy beach which rises gently towards the mountains of Moab.

This point becomes a natural meeting place for travellers. Mountain folk and Galilean fishermen wade across the Jordan to join the Judean artisans and Jerusalem businessmen. They make themselves comfortable among the reed-beds and beneath the carob trees. They come in search of John, the great preacher.

John, the only son of Zacharias, followed the custom of his day and left the easy life of the Temple in search of his calling. In the loneliness of these desert hills, he cultivated a strong, austere spirit.

And now the wasteland of Bethabara is both his sanctuary and his classroom . . .[7]

All Israel has come to see this man called 'the spirit

of Elijah'.[8] They have gathered here at the end of a difficult journey to hear this new preacher. If God, after four centuries of silence,[9] chooses to talk through this prophet, they all want to hear him.

Little by little, various groups begin to form. A short distance away, as if to remain aloof, stand the men of renown; the land-owning aristocracy and priestly classes. In their grasp they hold political and priestly power. Many possess noble titles. They live off the taxes, and the people both mistrust their astuteness and envy their wealth. Herodians[10] and Sadducees,[11] they control the Sanhedrin,[12] conspire with Herod, and spy for Pilate. They believe John to be a political agitator.

On the other side of the crowd, the Pharisees[13] stand apart. They represent learning and law. Among them are scribes, educated men, rabbis, doctors, teachers, barristers, theologians and judges. They study, think, write, and influence the opinions of the masses. They stand together, securely wrapped in culture, and middle-class respectability. Here to monitor events, they are determined to safeguard the status quo. Their arrogant self-sufficiency is, perhaps, the most hostile resistance confronting John the Baptist.

Roman soldiers patrol the area. Their swords and shields shimmer in the sun.[14] Perhaps a few of the senior officers who are here today were at the massacre of Bethlehem's children. Certainly, even the youngest among them has already participated in at least one crucifixion. Hardened by such cruelty, they shove people out of their way as they push through the crowd. Some of them, far from home, are off duty and have come out of curiosity, looking for a way to fill another empty day. Or, perhaps, they are searching for something. . . .

Undoubtedly, Zealots hide among the crowd.[15] They fight for freedom from Roman oppression. Idealistic and cruel, they can save a life or take it for the good of their cause. They conceal daggers beneath their robes; but their eyes glare fiercely. The authorities call them terrorists. They represent the national conscience; and the people fear them, admire them and protect them. They come to the Jordan, driven by their thirst for liberty and justice. John, too, speaks out against the abuses of the elite, against government corruption and clerical quislings. Could he be the leader, the messiah, who will free the nation?[16]

Near the water a small circle of publicans congregate.[17] Tax collectors, customs officials and accountants, they collaborate with the Romans for personal gain. They are looked upon as traitors. They are the creatures of the occupying power, living symbols of the hated Imperial authority. They have been rejected by the synagogue and the people, and they see in John their last hope for acceptance.

Women of burlesque beauty and skimpy dress join the publicans. Hated by some and exploited by others they, along with the publicans, feel excluded by society. They mingle with the riff-raff and the middle classes because loneliness engenders sadness. A little company for a little money. . . .[18] They, too, ache for respect, understanding and help. From a position of rock-bottom self-esteem, they dream of a better life.

A man in a white habit passes by. Maybe he comes from the Essene monastery which lies hidden among the desert hills of Qumran. He has rejected everything except piety, scholarship, and asceticism. He lives within the shadows of the monastery, far from the human needs and problems of the present.[19] Absorbed in self, he moves silently through the crowd. The loud laughter of children playing nearby startles him. Is it possible that in all his years of deprivation and isolation he has forgotten how laughter sounds? As his eyes focus on the children, a half-smile flickers across his face. Afraid of his own humanness, he pulls his habit closer and edges away. His life is a form of sectarianism, somewhere between that of the militant and the isolationist.

Townsmen, housewives with their children, and labourers swell the crowd along with the homeless, the beggars and the sick. Each has his own story. Each has his own family problems and personal conflicts. He comes with his loves and hates, his fears and frustrations — and his wounds.

Two fishermen, John and Andrew, come to hear the

preacher. A woman named Mary, of doubtful character, stands in the crowd along with a young lawyer who worries over his future. There is also a banker with a shady background, a hopelessly sick man who believes he is possessed by the devil, and some strong young men in search of a dream. These mix among the masses of the curious, indifferent, nervous, or resigned. Not much different from the rest, they would like to escape from their mediocrity. No longer satisfied with the dead-end streets of their past, they come looking for hope. They know, somehow, that life should mean more than just idleness and work, frivolity and suffering.

When the Baptist appears on the rocks, silence spreads over the crowd. His face glows with the radiance of heaven. When he begins to speak, his voice rings out strong and sure. He preaches his message with conviction and power. His voice echoes among the hills and resounds through the valley.

John cannot be bought. He does not fear the government, the clergy or the people. He preaches as one who tells the truth, condemning the sins of the common man and the crimes of the powerful.[20] He presents his message so directly that it cannot be misunderstood.

'The Kingdom of God is near. Messiah is coming. Prepare your hearts to receive Him.'

Strong in spirit, but sensitive in nature, John knows the suffering and the injustices endured by his hearers. He feels the profound depths of their sorrows. And his words condemn and terrorize some while they bring comfort and hope to others. John's words are those of a preacher of hope.[21]

He quotes Isaiah,[22] comparing his listeners to the surrounding desert: 'You are a rocky wasteland which must be cleared to make a highway for "the one who is to come". The Lord comes as a farmer to clean the threshing floor, to gather the wheat into His barn, to burn up the chaff.[23] He comes as a King to visit His subjects. "Prepare the way for the Lord, make straight paths for Him."'[24]

His message pierces the minds and consciences of his listeners. It awakens some from their complacency and challenges the fanaticism of others. And, in many, it sparks a spiritual longing. These ask themselves: 'What will the Messiah do with us when He comes? Are we wheat or chaff, rocky wasteland or cleared highway?'

Next, John addresses the Pharisees and the Sadducees. He knows that they have closed their minds to any type of reform.

'You brood of vipers! Who warned you to flee from the coming wrath? . . . The axe is already at the root of the trees, and every tree that does not produce good fruit will be cut down and thrown into the fire.'[25]

His anger fades and his flashing eyes soften as he gazes down upon the homeless and the sick. When he finally speaks, his voice trembles with emotion. Yet it rebounds off the rocks as a cry for liberty.

'Your King is coming to you. Fix the highway to your heart. He comes to relieve your suffering, to bind up your wounds and to break your bonds. Prepare the way for your God.'

Those despised by the virtuous recognize their need and respond first.

'"What should we do?"' the publicans ask.[26]

'Don't be greedy. Don't rob the people. Learn to be compassionate.'

A soldier pushes his way through the crowd.

'How can I wash away all the bloodstains? How can I forget the horror of it all? How can I be rid of the nightmares? What must I do?'[27]

John replies quickly, yet fearlessly: 'Begin to treat men as your brothers. Don't use unnecessary force. Life was never meant to be lived violently.'

'"What should we do?"' still others ask.[28]

'You must stop living selfishly. Share with those who have less. Be generous as your God has been with you.'

The powerful voice fills the air:

'Repent![29] Change your direction! Stop going in circles in the desert and start moving towards the Promised Land, following in the steps of the Saviour who will come.[30] We have all sinned. We all need cleansing.[31] Baptism symbolizes purification, death to our past and the beginning of a new life.[32] If you want to demonstrate your desire for a new life in God, come down to the water.'

John stops talking. The silence descends with him into the river. Some feel fire burning within their souls. They feel the seeds of life and hope germinating within their hearts.

After a moment's hesitation a soldier drops his sword and enters the river. A publican follows. Behind him come two women. And finally some young men walk resolutely to the river-bank. But something stops them. . . .

A young man is suddenly centre stage. They don't remember seeing him step out of the crowd. He lowers his tunic to the ground, revealing the muscular frame of an athlete — or perhaps a labourer. Something different about him draws the attention of the people. His young face, toughened and tanned, reflects serenity, nobility, purity and strength. Next to him, John the Baptist appears small and insignificant.

John stands paralysed for a moment. Then he turns towards the stranger and, grasping the man's hands in his, falls on his knees in the water.

'This is the long-awaited Messiah, the Saviour of the world. You must follow Him, not me. This is the One I was talking about when I said, "He comes after me, but he is greater than I am, because he existed before I was born."'[33]

John looks up into Jesus' eyes as he continues: 'I need to be baptized by you, and do you come to me? I baptize with water, but you will baptize us with the Holy Spirit.'[34]

But Jesus lifts John to his feet.

'John, today I begin my special ministry. I come to love men back to God. Help me to do everything according to the Divine Plan.'[35]

Trembling. John lowers Jesus into the water.[36] The sky opens and a white light surrounds the pair, embracing them in its warmth. A thunderclap booms in the sky and a majestic Voice rolls across the desert: 'This is my Son, whom I love; with him I am well pleased.'[37]

The light dims and as the Voice fades into the hills

beyond, Jesus steps from the water, retrieves His tunic, and makes His way through the shocked and silent crowd.

As He passes nearby, His sparkling eyes fall upon those who have come in search of life's meaning. He smiles at them, and they know that He has come as their Brother. They know that He has prayed for them. There in the Jordan He prayed that they would feel again the warmth of God's love. He prayed that they would let the waters of forgiveness wash them. He prayed that they, too, would hear God's voice say, 'You are my beloved child. I am satisfied with you.'

Jesus came; and returned to them in one moment the love that they had been missing for so long. And although He disappeared into the mountains of the desert after His baptism, they believed that they had found the Teacher for whom they had been searching. They knew that only He could fill the void within their hearts. They knew that they must find Him again.[38]

---

[1] My descriptions of the landscape are not mere literary creations. They are based on notes taken during visits to these places. Since each person sees the world from his own point of view, impressions are subjective. However, I have tried to remain accurate in my account of the surroundings.

[2] According to Jewish sources, the depression of the Dead Sea resulted from the destruction of Sodom and that region (cf. Gen. 10:19; 13:10, 11; chapters 18, 19. Sanhedrin 109). Others place this ancient, wicked city in the location of Mount Sedom, a hill of potassium to the northeast of what the Talmud calls 'the Sea of Sodom' (Shab. 108b). Others refer to the salt mountain called Sodom which is found to the south. The exact location is unknown (Encyclopaedia Judaica, Keter, Jerusalem, 1972, t. 15, cols. 70-72). Regarding Sodom's punishment, see Sanhedrin 109. This area has always been a centre of attention since ancient times owing to its high levels of salts, and for its surprising abundance of bitumen or asphalt. (Pausanias, Periegesis 5:7, 4, 5; Aristotle, Meteorologicum, 2:3, 29; Strabo, Geography 5:2, 41; Galenus, De simplicium medicamentorum facultatibus, 4:20).

[3] Jericho (the oldest city in Israel) was situated a little more than four miles west of the Jordan river, along the route to Jerusalem and on the edge of the most fertile oasis of the country.

[4] The gospels call this place Bethabara (John 1:28), Bethany (John 3:23) or Aenon, near Salim. It is a deserted place and the exact spot cannot be identified for certain.

[5] According to some of the oldest documents, the crossing of the Jordan river occurred in front of or near Jericho (Num. 22:1; Josh. 3:14-17; 4:1-9; 18-24; j Kiláyim 9:5).

16 IN THE DESERT

⁶See 2 Kgs 2:1-15.

⁷Luke 1:13-17. The prophecy recorded in Malachi 4:5, 6 announced that Elijah would come before the Messiah. Jesus referred to John the Baptist as 'the Elijah who is to come' (Matt. 11:14; 17:10-13; Mark 9:11-13), although later He refused to identify John in this way before the scribes in order to avoid confusion about reincarnation (John 1:19-28). Regarding the waiting for 'the spirit of Elijah' as the precursor of the Messiah, see *Zabim* 48:10-11; *Berakoth* 35b; *Menahoth* 45a; *Bekoroth* 24a; *Eduyot* 8:7.

⁸For more information about John's ministry in the desert, see Matt. 3:1-12; 11:7-14; Mark 1:4-8; Luke 3:1-20; 7:24-30. The fact that a young man went to the desert to live alone for a time was a practice rooted in the religion of the day. It was a common practice to leave family and friends for a time in order to find oneself or God. Flavius Josephus, the well-known Jewish historian, told how in his youth, after he had looked in vain for answers to his religious questions in the different veins of thought of his time, he had followed a hermit named Bannus who lived off wild plants and fruits near the Jordan. (*Life*, 2.) John the Baptist followed the same procedure before beginning his ministry (Luke 1:80), as did Jesus (Mark 1:12, 13), and Saul of Tarsus (Gal. 1:17).

⁹The 'prophetic silence' in Israel had lasted for more than four centuries (according to the rabbinical tradition, based on Psalm 74:9).

¹⁰Those few supporters of the Idumean dynasty of the Herods were called Herodians. Generally, they were government workers and officials who occupied high public offices. The orthodox Jews considered the dynasty to be usurpers, since the royal family did not originate among the Hebrews (Josephus, *Ant.* 15:15, 2), cf. Matt. 22:16; Mark 3:6; 12:13.

¹¹According to Josephus (*Ant.* 13:293), the Sadducees came from the highest classes. They did not recognize any authority other than that of the Pentateuch (the Law of Moses), and rejected the prophets and the prophetic books. Among their beliefs, their denial of life beyond death stands out (*War* 2:165; Mark 12:18-27; Matt. 22:23; Luke 20:27; Acts 23:6-8). Since, according to their thinking, they had only one life, they identified prosperity with Divine approval, and poverty or misfortune with Divine punishment or curse. Their own affluence was their best argument that they had received God's blessings (*Ant.* 18:16-17)!

¹²The Sanhedrin (a Greek word meaning 'to sit together') was a type of State tribunal which was created after the exile. It was made up of seventy-one members (perhaps in memory of Moses and the seventy elders of Exod. 24:1 and Num. 11:16). Most were Sadducees (priests and representatives of the nobility). From the days of Queen Alexandra (77-67BC) the Pharisees began to be represented as well, by the most renowned scribes (cf. Matt. 5:22; 26:59; Mark 14:55; 15:1; Luke 22:66; John 11:47; Acts 5:21-41; 6:12-15; 22:30; 23:1-28).

¹³Pharisee, in Aramaic (perishayya), means 'the separated one'. This term, known to exist from 235BC, was used to identify someone who separated himself from something. It could mean the one who separated himself from government protection, or from sin by rigorous religious practice, as

well as those who separated themselves from society in order to preserve their holiness, and even those who separated from the traditional interpretation of the Law. Josephus compares his attitudes and beliefs to those of the Stoics (*Life* 12). The Talmud is the most important perpetration of the Pharisaical spirit. For more information regarding their life-style, see *War* 1:5; 2:8; and all of book 13; cf. Mark 12:13-17; Matt. 23:1-36 and Luke 11:37-54. The scribes were the official interpreters of the Law and were generally Pharisees. Josephus, although a Pharisee himself, emphasized their legalism (*Ant.* 18:1).

[14] From the year 63BC, Palestine was under Roman occupation and dependent on the province of Syria (Josephus, *Ant.* 14:66-74). The Romans preferred to rule through Idumean princes or governors who presented less risk of national uprisings since they themselves were not Jews. The Roman strength depended upon the legions. The hardness and cruelty of the Roman army was evident in the massacre of the children of Bethlehem (Matt. 2:13-18), and that of the Galileans (Luke 13:1); not to mention the torture of crucifixion (Luke 23:11-26, 36, 37).

[15] The Zealot movement against the Roman oppression began with Judas of Galilee (Josephus, *War* 2:56; 2:118; cf. Acts 5:37). Two of his sons, Jacob and Simon, were crucified by order of the procurate, Tiberius Alexander, in the year AD 47 (Josephus, *Ant.* 20:102) and another man named Menahem took by force the stronghold of Masada in the year AD 66, at the beginning of the national revolt. They resisted the Romans until the year AD 74. Josephus calls certain types of terrorists 'sicarius'. These were armed with sharp knives (sica), and took advantage of crowds to stab their victims with such speed that they were rarely caught. (*War* 2:254. There are some who associate the name Judas Iscariot with 'sicarius'.) One of the most famous acts of zealotry was the burning of the financial records of the temple, where all the debts were recorded. They did that in order to gain the sympathy of the poor and indebted during the uprising against the Romans in the year AD 60. (*War* 2:427.)

[16] Although the expectations regarding the Messiah were diverse and contradictory, depending upon the different religious tendencies, in the first century all expected that the Messiah would lift the Roman yoke, unify Israel, and rule the world (*Psalms of Solomon* 17:25-28).

[17] Rather than being government employees the publicans were businessmen hired by the State to collect taxes. They purchased their position and worked out ways to make it a profitable investment. (For more about the financial oppression of the time, see Josephus, *Ant.* 18:274). They were hated by the people because they collaborated with the oppressive Roman government. The religious classes hated them because they transgressed the sacred laws which regulated the charging of interest (Exod. 22:25; Lev. 25:36, 37; Deut. 23:20, 21; *Sanhedrin* 25b). The rabbis maintained that 'it was difficult for a publican to obtain pardon' (*Baba Kamma* 94b) since it was nearly impossible to find all those whom they had cheated in order to repay them (cf. Luke 18:9-14). The term 'publican' is always

associated with 'sinners' in every text from this time-period (Matt. 9:10, 11; 11:19; Mark 2:15, 16; Luke 7:34; 15:1, 2). It is also associated with 'pagans' (Matt. 18:17), and 'harlots' (Matt. 21:31, 32).

[18] Although prostitution was prohibited by the law of Moses (Deut. 23:17, 18), especially among the daughters of the priests (Lev. 21:9), in practice it was tolerated and even protected, since a relationship with a prostitute was not considered to be adultery. For that reason, prostitutes worked publicly from the earliest of Bible times (Gen. 38:13-26; Prov. 5; 6:24-26; 7:5-27). They were easily recognized by their way of dressing (Prov. 7:10). For more details about the prostitute's 'way of dressing' see Ezek. 16:8-63; Isa. 3:16-24. According to Josephus (Ant. 4:8) neither those women nor their descendants could participate in the religious community of Israel.

[19] Regarding the austerity of the Essene monasteries, see Josephus (War 2:137-139); and about their incredible frugality (2:129-133). The severity of their code of conduct is revealed in The Community Rule (1QS) 6:24-8:25. A case of fraud or of lying, for example, could be punished by the reduction of the food ration; (which consisted only of bread and water) to one-fourth for the rest of life. Laughing or sleeping during a meeting could result in ten days of solitary confinement. Pliny describes an Essene monastery near the Dead Sea (Naturalis Historia 5:73). The discoveries of Qumran have allowed us to understand the beliefs and life-styles of that desert community. Philo of Alexandria talks about their passiveness towards life (or impassiveness) and says that 'we would search in vain among them for someone who would dedicate himself to create . . . even good objects for fear that they might be used for evil' (Quid omnis probus liber sit 78).

[20] For more information regarding the corruption in Herod's court, see Josephus (Ant. 15:259; 17:349-353; 18:136; 20:143). According to Mark 6:17-29, John the Baptist was beheaded at Herod's command, in the midst of an orgy, owing to the fact that he had dared to condemn the sinful relationship of the monarch with his sister-in-law (cf. Lev. 18:16). According to Josephus, Herod feared John the Baptist and looked upon him as an agitator who would stir up the people against him (Ant. 18:116, 117).

[21] Josephus describes John the Baptist's preaching in this way: 'John, called the Baptist, is an exceptional man. He teaches that the Jews should endeavour to do good; that is, to be just with others and to honour God. In addition, they should be baptized; although, according to his teachings, the baptism is only valid before God if the baptized one is already justified within by his just behaviour; (the baptism) justifies the body but does not save one from sin' (Ant. 18:5, 2).

[22] Isa. 40:3-5 (cf. Luke 3:4-6).
[23] Luke 3:17, 18.
[24] Matt. 3:1-3, NIV.
[25] Matt. 3:5-10, NIV.
[26] Luke 3:12, 13, NIV.
[27] Luke 3:14.
[28] Luke 3:10, 11, NIV.
[29] Matt. 3:2. The Greek word which is translated 'repent' is 'metanoeite'

which means, literally, 'change your mind, or your way of thinking'. This term is usually translated into the Hebrew root 'shuv' which means to 'return', or to 'turn back' on the wrong road in order to take the correct way. The thought in both languages is similar: it refers to a change in orientation; an existential decision which does not mean reviewing all the previous sins (as the words 'repent' or 'penitence' might suggest and which undoubtedly refer to remorse). Rather, it means turning around to find the Saviour.

[30] It is interesting to note that the texts refer to the place where John baptized as being 'beyond the Jordan' (John 1:28; 10:40); that is, beside the Jordan. If John baptized in the Jordan, why then this insistence in designating the place as being on the other side? The fact that he set himself up in a historically famous site suggests that John wanted to symbolize with the baptism the 'crossing of the Jordan' spiritually, going from the deserted past to the new reality of the Promised Land under the leadership of the new Joshua. (In Hebrew, Jesus and Joshua are the same name.)

[31] The biblical teaching that evil 'contaminates' (see Rom. 5:12-21) deserves to be examined. In the same way that lack of respect for natural laws results in ecological imbalance, deterioration of health and life, and finally contamination and destruction, the lack of respect for the laws which govern human behaviour (in biblical terms, the transgression of the principles of conduct revealed in God's Law) results in psychological imbalance, moral decadence, spiritual deterioration, social contamination; and, finally, destruction of human coexistence.

[32] The New Testament describes baptism as a 'sign of regeneration' (Titus 3:5); as a 'new birth' (John 3:5); as a 'death and resurrection' with Christ (Rom. 6:3-6; Col. 2:12); and as 'an appeal to God for a clear conscience' (1 Peter 3:21).

[33] John 1:15, 29-34; 3:22-36.

[34] Matt. 3:11, 13-15; John 1:26, 27.

[35] Matt. 3:13-15 says that Jesus wanted to be baptized ' "to fulfil all righteousness" ' (RSV), an enigmatic phrase which seems to indicate 'to fulfil the Divine Plan'.

[36] The term 'to baptize' comes from a Greek word which means 'to submerge in water' (Homer, *Odyssey* 9:392; Aeschylus, *Prometheus* 863), and could stand for a body to be washed (Menander, *Fragmenta* 363:4), clothing to be washed or dyed (Josephus, *War* 4:563; *Ant.* 3:102), or any other object to be submerged (*War* 3:368). Baptism consisted of the total immersion of the convert in the water. John baptized at Aenon, near Salim, 'because there was plenty of water' (John 3:23). The baptismal rite carries full significance only when it is by full immersion. This is made clear in some versions of the New Testament.

[37] Matt. 3:16, 17; Mark 1:9-11; Luke 3:21, 22; John 1:29-34.

[38] The three synoptic gospels agree that immediately after His baptism Jesus withdrew to the desert (Matt. 4:1; Mark 1:12; Luke 4:1). The search for Jesus by John's disciples is documented in John 1:35-42.

In the night

Deserted streets stare at him in sinister silence. Wrapped tightly in his cape so as not to be recognized as he crosses through the pale white moonlight,[1] he cautiously steps out of the darkened doorway. Life in the great city has taught him to distrust the shadowy portals. Yet he prefers the darkness to the ridicule he will face if caught rendezvousing with the young Teacher.

Jesus' peculiar style fascinates and frightens him. No one has ever displayed such a powerful and independent personality. Who else would be so bold, so forward, as to chase the merchants from the Temple?[2]

Nicodemus recalls the many teachers to whom he has listened in his spiritual quest. This man's ideas do not come from any of the common schools of thought nor from any known sect or political party. Jesus' magnetic spirituality sparks Nicodemus' professional curiosity. He decides that he must discover this man's secret.[3]

But approaching Jesus poses a difficult and compromising act. Nicodemus has spent his entire life preparing to be a doctor of the law.[4] An excellent student in the rabbinical schools and now a powerful Pharisee, he is known for his knowledge of the Scriptures. He even holds a coveted seat on the Sanhedrin. To be seen consulting with this itinerant preacher would be to risk his reputation as a scholar.

After some careful thought, Nicodemus chooses to meet Jesus at night in an obscure place. In order to avoid feeling intimidated by a visit which could become too personal, he approaches Jesus as the representative of a group who share his ideas. Nicodemus does in fact, have friends who look with sympathy upon the Galilean. But they, too, fear risking position and honour and have chosen to remain in the shadows.[5]

Nicodemus has reached the rendezvous. Here, in front of Jesus, he seems to forget for a moment his social status. Here at last he senses that he can allow his inmost feelings of unrest to surface. He seems to know that with Jesus he can admit that nagging feeling of emptiness which has been with him for so long. In a spirit of humility rarely seen in men of his class, he addresses this country carpenter as Rabbi or 'Teacher'.

The essence of this conversation, undoubtedly deep and engaging, takes only half a page in the gospel of John.[6]

' "Rabbi, we know you are a teacher who has come from God, for no one could perform the miraculous signs you are doing if God were not with him." '[7]

Taking no notice of Nicodemus' flattery and dispensing with protocol, Jesus accepts His role as teacher. He begins to present Nicodemus with ideas which will force him to re-evaluate his entire way of thinking.[8]

Jesus begins by challenging Nicodemus' Pharisaical ideas: 'I tell you the truth, unless a man is born again, he cannot see the Kingdom of God. That is, if you want your world to change, first *you* must change.'

Nicodemus takes a step back. What does Jesus mean? It is true that many things must be corrected and changed in order to make the world a better place. He wants great change. He longs for the Messiah's appearing and for the liberation of Israel and a prosperous kingdom under the Divine blessing. He has come to Jesus to find out how he, as a national leader, can accelerate its coming.[9] Even his name (Victory for the People)[10] reveals his desire for change.

But the idea of a new birth from above, of a new beginning,[11] stops him in his tracks. He does not see any relationship between the desired change in world affairs and his own way of life. A complete transformation, a radical personal change, seems not only impossible but unnecessary. He is, after all, Nicodemus — honest, sincere, religious, respected, admired and appreciated.

Must one really become a different person, with other ideals, other goals, much higher than those held before? Cannot anything be salvaged? Is it even possible to break away from the past and begin again with better principles?

If he understands Jesus correctly, then he must abandon even the most sure and indisputable of his beliefs, his religious ideals. Does this mean that religious piety, even devotion as faithful as his, will not suffice? That such faithfulness is not enough to enter 'the Kingdom of God'?

Nicodemus, good Pharisee that he is, believes that man can save himself through obedience to the Divine laws.[12] Is there a Kingdom too pure for even him to enter? Must he admit that he needs a new life rather than new religious practices? Must he admit that he is a spiritual embryo when he has imagined himself upon the peak of spiritual maturity? Isn't it all a bit excessive?

Nicodemus cannot understand what Jesus is saying. Every man is a slave of his past: a slave to his family upbringing, his social background, to unique circumstances which have, to a great extent, conditioned his responses. No one can forget his past, break with everything, and begin again.

But Jesus insists: 'Not even the best heritage, the most advantageous surroundings, or the most exclusive religious education can guarantee entrance into the superior realm of reality which we call "the Kingdom of God". None of this is sufficient because the reality is quite simply to allow God to reign unconditionally within us.[13] And we are so far from allowing Him this privilege that to do so really would mean being "born again" or "from above".'

'To be "born from above" is to begin to live fully. We are marred and limited because we are humans. We are not born totally alive. From the moment of birth we carry deep within us death's seed. To be born from above means reaching the summit of human existence through the restoration of a lost spiritual dimension. It means shedding the thick skin that envelopes and encloses us, forcing us to see that our small world is not the sole reality. It means opening our eyes to the light of another, better world. It means discovering that by connecting ourselves to God even our limitations can be overcome.

Nicodemus feels dizziness creeping over him. This teaching, if he follows it, will force him to abandon his conventional beliefs and attitudes. Fighting to preserve his point of reference, he controls himself through sheer mental discipline and sarcastically challenges Jesus' idea as simplistically absurd: 'How can a man be born when he is old?'

Is Nicodemus old, or does he feel erroneously that it is too late for him to start again?

His rejection does not stem from stupidity nor bad intentions. Rather, it is the defensive mechanism of a man whose belief-system has been threatened. It is the response of a frightened, yet honest, intellect. Nicodemus needs to test the ground before stepping on to it.

He cannot understand from his human perspective how God can change a man and yet respect his freedom of choice. His private interview with Jesus will teach him that the idea of being born again is less absurd than that of trying to save himself by his own efforts. Jesus will show him that he can have an infinitely greater guarantee of success if he responds to the all-embracing power of God rather than trusting in his own limited resources. Nicodemus doesn't understand that Jesus is not requiring the impossible but offering the seemingly unattainable; that the new birth is not something that Christ requires of Nicodemus; but a gift He is prepared to bestow on him, fully and generously.

In the spiritual realm the 'self-made man' does not exist. Man is incapable of rebuilding without help from outside. To begin from ground-level is beyond his capabilities. To begin a truly new life, he must first experience his own helplessness and his need for outside intervention.

In the face of Nicodemus' incomprehension, Jesus states the same thing in different words: 'I tell you the truth, unless a man is born of water and the Spirit, he cannot enter the kingdom of God.'

For an expert in the Scriptures, the mention of 'water' and 'Spirit' is a clear allusion to the principles of creation.[14] The new birth signifies a new creation. That is, the action is not human but divine.

Jesus explains: 'In mankind there are two levels of existence: the 'carnal' and the 'spiritual'. Each can transmit only the life that it possesses. The flesh transmits the weak human condition. The spirit transmits the power of God.

'Human aspirations reach no higher than economic well-being, family satisfaction, or personal prestige. From this level man can never hope to become all that God has planned him to be, nor can he overcome his own innate weaknesses.

'Flesh gives birth to flesh, but the Spirit gives birth to spirit.[15] Man can defeat his spiritual impotence only with God's power.'

The new birth suggested by Jesus means entering into a new reality whose centre is God and not man. It means passing from a life of dependence, restricted and choked by human limitations, to a life free and open to all the possibilities of the Spirit. It means passing from the reality of condemnation and death to the vibrancy of new life.

Surprised by Jesus' language, Nicodemus asks how this change is possible.

With slight irony, Jesus forces him to look for life's meaning outside the bounds of his religious upbringing. 'You are Israel's teacher . . . and you do not understand these things?'

Nicodemus knows so much. Religion is his area of expertise. He moves in a world of theological debate and argument. He stands out as a learned scholar. But somehow he has missed the most elementary of lessons. He has not learned that the spiritual life depends not upon his own theological knowledge about God but upon his relationship with Him. He has not learned that a person can obtain the high title of Doctor of the sacred Scriptures without a personal relationship with the God revealed in Scripture.

'You should not be surprised,' Jesus continues, 'at My saying, "You must be born again." The wind blows wherever it pleases. You hear its sound, but you cannot tell where it comes from or where it is going. So it is with everyone born of the Spirit.'

'The spiritual rebirth changes violent men into apostles of peace. Men formerly consumed by hatred can forgive and love. The erstwhile mean, self-indulgent, and egotistical person volunteers his services in the most generous enterprises. . . . One doesn't need to understand the process of regeneration. The important thing is that it occurs, and for it to occur we must respond to the love of God in our hearts, constraining us to surrender to Him. The powerful energy of grace supplies the rest. No one knows how it occurs. But in a given moment, it breaks into our lives and transforms us. The new birth cannot be explained. It can only be experienced. And not just once for all time, but each and every day.'[16]

Nicodemus finally discovers how shallow is his knowledge of God. He has tried to understand from his own point of reference, but Divine Creativity cannot be enclosed within the framework of theology. The fault does not lie in his sources but in his interpretation. The Old Testament is a continual lesson on the incredible initiative of Divine Love. But just as it is difficult for the materialist to imagine a reality apart from things, the legalist cannot imagine a relationship with God other than in terms of obedience to law.

Nicodemus reveals his confusion when he asks, 'How can this be?'

These are his last recorded words during that night encounter. From here on, Nicodemus listens in silence to this unusual Friend without interrupting. Jesus tells him: '"We speak of what we know, and we testify to what we have seen."'[17]

Nicodemus came looking for a messiah to rule over Israel. But God has decided to rule over all mankind. His Envoy will be king over all who wish to be born into a life without end in a kingdom of love without frontiers: '"For God so loved the world that he gave his one and only Son, that whoever believes in him shall not perish but have eternal life."'[18]

If God loves without barriers and wishes us happiness without limits, His objective when He sent the Messiah could not have been the judgement, as Nicodemus and his colleagues believed.[19] The judgement would be the ultimate consequence of human freedom. The mission of the Son was to bring life; now and forever. His aim was not to destroy some and save others, but to bring hope to all.

He prefers volunteers to pawns who are forced into compliance. His kingdom cannot be established by force, but by loving persuasion.

Jesus reads Nicodemus' mind as he wonders, 'What must one do to have this life. How can one be born again?' Man, suffering from a death blow deep within, need only grasp the new life as one with a serious wound pins his hope on any available cure.

'"Just as Moses lifted up the snake in the desert, so the Son of Man must be lifted up, that everyone who believes may have eternal life in him."'[20]

The human race condemned itself to death by separating from God, the only Source of life. Our only chance of survival is to connect our mortality with eternity. Our destiny depends upon acceptance. To give in to the Light of Life or to separate ourselves in pursuit of the clouds of nothingness: there are no other choices. In some dangerous births, the only solution is surgical intervention. So we, too, can see the light only through the intervention of the Surgeon 'from above'. A radical solution; but in just such a solution is our salvation.

'"Whoever lives by the truth comes into the light."'[21]

With these words of hope echoing in his ears, Nicodemus leaves. This restless intellectual has found more than a teacher. However, though he leaves marked forever by this disconcerting message, it will take time before he will act on what he has learned. His will not be a rapid 'birth' but a prolonged 'gestation'.

He could have become a new man that night, entering into the service of the Gospel. Instead, he continued to keep the law as a means of earning salvation.

Nicodemus waited three years before making his decision. Only when the Sanhedrin decided to arrest and finish once and for all with this revolutionary Preacher did Nicodemus finally risk himself in the Teacher's defence.[22] He waited, not for lack of conviction, but courage. Too afraid of what others would think and of how a decision for Jesus would affect his career, he admired from a distance. He ran the risk of never leaving the lukewarm group which God will eventually spit from His mouth.[23] He waited until he saw Jesus hanging on the cross that terrible Friday.[24]

Finally, remembering Jesus' allusion to the serpent lifted up in the wilderness, he dared to stand and declare himself for the crucified Jesus. Defying leaders and colleagues whom he had always feared, he asked for the body of Jesus, and as a final tribute to One whom he had followed only from afar, he covered with perfume the wounds that his own cowardice had helped to inflict.

After meeting Jesus that first night, Nicodemus returned to his own world. But, beyond the shadows, in the distant horizon of his life, an inescapable sunrise had begun to dawn.

---

¹The Gospel of John (3:1-17) places this event just after the first Passover of Jesus' public ministry (2:13-23). Since the feast began with the full moon of spring (the 14th day of the lunar month) and lasted seven days more (Exod. 12:1-28), the meeting between Jesus and Nicodemus could have taken place towards the end of the days of unleavened bread or a little later.

²John 2:13-22.

³The rabbinical teachings were based upon their faithfulness to the authority of tradition. These writings became known as the Mishna (oral interpretations of the laws of the Torah, compiled by rabbis in the second century) and the Talmud (a commentary of the Mishna which became the civil and religious code for Israel). Rabbi Eliezer resisted those who tried to force him to say 'anything which he had not heard from his master'. (Sukkah 27b.) Rabbi Jose ben Juda said, 'I have never in my life said a thing which I did not hear from my teachers.' (Sukkah 28a.) The Talmudic writings often begin in the following way:

'It has been said that Rabbi Isaac ben Joseph said in R. Johanan's name that the tradition to follow is that which R. Juda ben Ahad, son of R. Huna said in R. Shesheth's name. . . .' (Baba Mezi'a. 33a).

We can imagine the impact produced by Jesus' teachings among those who held that 'he who interprets the Torah in a different way from the traditional (Halakha) will be cursed' (Sanhedrin 99a) and that 'the true teacher is the one who doesn't take any credit upon himself'. (Aboth 6.)

Jesus surprised His listeners, among other reasons, 'because He taught as one Who had authority and not as the scribes' (Matt. 7:29; Mark 1:22). Even the temple guards who were sent to arrest Him returned without laying a hand on Him, saying, 'Never have we heard a man speak as this man.' John 7:46.

⁴John 3:1. At the end of long studies, at the age of 40, the student was ordained as a scribe. That gave him jurisdictional authority, especially in the Sanhedrin where he occupied a seat by right (Sanhedrin 11:3; Matt. 26:57).

⁵John 2:23-25, NIV.

⁶John 3:1-21.

⁷John 3:2, NIV.

⁸Nicodemus' spiritual problem becomes apparent in his use of the term 'we know'. He felt secure in his religious culture and knowledge, but in reality he knew much less than he imagined.

⁹The Jewish uprising against the Romans in the years AD66-70 was

unleashed by a resistance movement headed by the youthful intellectuals among the Pharisees and Zealots (Josephus, *War* 2:117 and ss.) They were convinced that 'God would only support their endeavour if man actively co-operated in it and if he did not abandon the great cause due to hardship' (*Ant.* 18:5).

[10] Nicodemus is a Greek name formed by Nike, which means 'victory', and demos, 'people'. Put together it signifies 'victory for the people'. The name reveals a liberal and nationalistic spirit since the strict Jews used Hebrew names of theological origin.

[11] The word *anothen* used in the Greek text signifies all of this.

[12] The central line of theological belief for the Pharisees was that obedience to the law was the only road to salvation, both on personal and national levels: 'Great is the Torah which gives to those who practise its commands life in this world and in the world to come' (*Abot* 6:7). 'The Torah is life . . . he who possesses its words possesses the future world' (2:8). Even the coming of the Messiah depended upon Israel's completion of the law: 'If Israel would obey the law perfectly for only one day, the Son of David would come immediately.' (J Ta'anith 64a). The obedience required included, along with the biblical laws, those added by tradition: 'Awesome are the words of the wise; to transgress them is worse than transgressing the words of the Scriptures' (*Midrash* on Deut. 17:11).

[13] For this reason Jesus can say that 'the Kingdom of God is among you'. (Luke 17:21.)

[14] Gen. 1:1-3.

[15] John 3:6. Jesus also refers to the symbolism of baptism. Behind the visible symbol (water) is the invisible (the spirit). The immersion of the believer symbolizes his death to his past life, and his breathing again on rising from the water symbolizes the living breath of the Spirit which fills the new life. The importance is not found in the ritual of the water. It is in the spiritual reality which introduces man into communion with God.

[16] 1 Cor. 15:31; 2 Cor. 4:16.

[17] John 3:9-11, NIV.

[18] John 3:16, NIV.

[19] Based upon the prophecy given in Daniel 7, it was believed Messiah's mission would be the liberation of Israel and the judgement of the nations, beginning with Rome. (*Abodah Zarah* 2 a, b.).

[20] John 3:14, 15, NIV; see Num. 21:4-9.

[21] John 3:21, NIV.

[22] John 7:40-52.

[23] Rev. 3:14-22.

[24] John 19:38-42.

By the well[1]

The sun blazes mercilessly in the midday sky. Sultry, stifling, and suffocating, the heat shimmer rises from the stones. A dusty traveller tries in vain to protect Himself from the sweltering rays. He sits alone in the plaza. At this hour everyone retreats to the cool darkness of his house.

Why has He chosen such a solitary time of the day to wait by the well?[2] He could have chosen the morning. At dawn a chill envelops the plaza, bravely challenging the rising sun. And in the evening the coolness steals back, almost imperceptibly at first, as shadows lengthen and the heat slowly subsides.

These are the hours when, all along the path, brown pitchers may be seen bobbing above the dark heads and white veils. Women's laughter fills the air. Boys, wishing to be men, cluster bashfully upon the stepping stones of the plaza, awaiting the maidens who come there to draw water. Men sit in the shadows, discussing politics and business. The well is the centre of town life at these times. But not now, at midday. So why is Jesus here?

Jesus trekked through Samaria to Sychar[3] in order to confront the pain and prejudice of human hearts.[4] Jesus knows that Jews and Samaritans share only the rivalry of separate religious ruins.[5] They share only the common ground of hatred, pride, arrogance and grudges.[6] Scarred by years of mistrust and insult, the people of these neighbouring countries will not even speak to one another. Today, Jesus chooses to reach beyond the hatred and the hurt to the hated and the hurting.

Jesus comes at noon because He knows the Samaritan woman will be there. He sits waiting.

She trudges up the hot, dusty path alone, accompanied only by her shadow. Her lonely arrogance is as visible as her bracelets glinting in the sun. No one knows what she hides behind her aggressive look, but her midday trips to the well have long been a topic of conversation among the townspeople.

She ignores the Stranger; but He has come to meet her. He addresses her in a way she is sure to understand: 'Give me a drink.'

The woman pauses. Why has this Jew spoken to her? What can he want from a Samaritan woman? His request is nothing more than an overworked line. Asking for water beside a well! Almost all the love stories in Sychar begin this way. When Abraham decided to give his son in marriage, he sent his servant to the well. His strategy was the same, way back then. '"May it be that when I say to a girl, 'Please let down your jar that I may have a drink,' and she says, 'Drink, and I'll water your camels too' — let her be the one you have chosen for your servant Isaac."'[7]

That was how Isaac and Rebecca came to be married. Today this strange Jew sits at the well which had been dug by Jacob, the son of that famous couple,[8] and asks her for a drink.

The Samaritan woman knows the line by heart. She has participated in the scenario alongside the well with five or six men, each time hoping that her dreams would finally come true. But that had been when she could still dream. Is this man any different? Can he offer her hope for the future? Will she encounter her destiny here today? Can she dream just once more?

She eyes Jesus cautiously, still unconvinced. Unwilling to trust again yet just as unwilling to end the conversation, she teasingly plays with her words. She speaks of water as one would speak of the rain when it is torrential or the sun when there is good weather. She speaks merely to fill the silence until she can decide what this stranger has to offer.

An abyss, seemingly impassable, separates Jesus from this woman. It separates their worlds, yet Jesus reaches out to her. Her world is one of unstable relationships in the night. Jesus presents her with an encounter at high noon.

He chooses His words carefully, each one calculated to spark hope where there is none. Apart from His genuine thirst, He knows that to ask for water is to say: 'I've come to talk about your future.' How else could He interest a woman like her?

'If you knew the gift of God and who it is that is saying to you, "Give me a drink," you would have asked Him and He would have given you living water which would never run dry; a water that overflows all boundaries and which cannot be channelled by any system of irrigation; a fountain of life, a spring of hope. This water which I have brings life to the spirit and to the body. It cleanses inside and out.'

It is not strange that, when Jesus offers the Samaritan better water, she thinks in concrete terms. Can this man offer her a house with a water storage tank? Can he offer her a tap, a sink, or perhaps even a bathroom of marble? No. He does not seem able to offer her any of these. And so the woman sidesteps involvement and continues to draw water.

Time is precious for Jesus. He already sees His returning disciples far away. And so He dispenses with the normal formalities of new acquaintances and offers her, from the depths of His human compassion, water much more valuable and refreshing. He speaks of 'living' water.[9] Jesus believes the Samaritan is capable of following the spiritual lesson.

By talking with her of spiritual things, Jesus shows her the respect not often shown to women of the time, and thus places her above social barriers, religious taboos, sexist exclusion and racial borders. He frees theology from its last strait-jacket and puts it to work on behalf of this woman. Will He be understood?

In order to clear up any misunderstanding, Jesus turns towards her once more and says: 'Go, call your husband and come back.' In this way He is really saying, 'Show me your true identity, your social status. Introduce me to the one who gives you a name and legal standing.'[10]

She responds quickly: 'I have no husband.'

'"You are right when you say you have no husband. The fact is, you have had five husbands, and the man you now have is not your husband. What you have just said is quite true."'[11]

Jesus does not condemn the woman. He speaks not of adultery nor divorce.[12] Neither is His simple statement meant to humour her. He simply reads her heart.

'Five husbands. Five unclosed wounds. How many disappointments you have suffered! It is not strange that in order to avoid more suffering you commit yourself less and less. You have buried five dreams. Five times you planted gardens where there was only desert. You cannot take more failure, but the ground is still parched. If you have given up on human love, could it be because you are actually looking for eternal acceptance?'

The woman begins to understand. 'Sir, I can see that you are a prophet.'

The Samaritan, for a brief moment, drops her mask of frivolity before the discernment of her strange acquaintance, allowing Him to glimpse the broken heart of a young girl. But she recovers quickly.

'I am not a practising believer, although I have always wanted to believe. But what should I believe in? You say that the Jews possess the truth. And your God can be worshipped only in your temple. But the Samaritans say that one can find God only in Mount Gerizim.'[13]

This quick-witted, intelligent woman knows that religions tend to envelop themselves in the cocoon of their own beliefs. She knows that the religious too often argue among themselves out of fervour, fanaticism and pride. She also knows that religious leaders are men.[14] As a Samaritan, the woman understands men only too well. . . . So she asks Jesus a question meant to draw Him from her own personal case to much less dangerous issues.

But Jesus sees through her strategy at once. And since His bias is neither towards the Jews nor the Samaritans, He avoids both options: 'God is higher than our ecclesiastical systems and larger than our theological debates. In order to find Him you need not make a pilgrimage to a temple or climb a mountain. You need only to search the depths of your own heart.[15]

'Religion without love as its core is nothing more than an empty cistern. To try to worship God without the indwelling spirit of truth is neither realistic nor, indeed, possible. For this reason, we find only emptiness in so many sanctuaries. They are no more than ancient dwellings on the verge of collapse. Only when we hunger and thirst after righteousness will we be satisfied, our thirst quenched. Only when we drink of living water can we truly find eternal life.'

The Samaritan woman sighs and says: 'I know that Messiah (called Christ) is coming. When He comes, He will explain everything to us.'[16]

Jesus answers, 'The time has come. I Who speak to you am He.'

The great revelation is made. Not to a dyed-in-the-wool Jew but to a foreigner. Not to a devout, pious woman, but to a lost soul. Jesus reveals Himself to the outcast. He offers the covenant to the scorned and thirsty one.

The Samaritan woman no longer dips for water in the same old well. By its edge she leaves her empty pitcher. She runs home to tell her neighbours about Jesus.

Today healing water has begun to flow. There is enough to cleanse all the wounds that the human heart has borne. Its abundance not only satisfies all Sychar and Samaria[17] but it runs free for all, healing wounds and quenching thirst wherever it goes.

---

[1]Text based on John 4:4-26. The setting is based on J. Debruyne, *Jesus*, Paris: Desclee, 1986, pages 121-136.

[2]Jacob's Well exists today and is preserved in a crypt of one of the churches of the Crusaders which is constructed upon the ruins of a Byzantine sanctuary from the fourth century.

[3]Sychar is probably the ancient Shechem, a town located between the famous mountains of Ebal and Gerizim. Destroyed in 128BC, in Roman times it was reconstructed about one mile from its primitive site and given the name of Flavia Neapolis.

[4]The sentence 'had to go through Samaria' (John 4:4) uses the term 'dei' as used in the gospels to underscore a deliberate action as part of a pre-established plan.

[5]Deut. 27:4-7 indicated that Mt. Ebal was to be a holy place of worship in the new land of Canaan. But based on the Divine commands of Deut. 11:29 and 27:12, which point to Mt. Gerizim as the mountain of blessings, the Samaritans sanctified Mt. Gerizim instead of Ebal. For the Jews there was only one Temple — that of Jerusalem.

[6]Among Jews of that period it was said, 'These are two nations that my soul hates, and a third that is not my people: the inhabitants of Mt. Seir, the Philistines and the foolish people of Shechem' (*The Book of Sirach* 50:25-26). Contact with Samaritans was avoided as much as or more than with pagans.

[7]Gen. 24.

[8] The well, named after Jacob, was located in the land which he gave to his son Joseph (Gen. 33:18-20; 48:22).

[9] Water, symbol of life (Ps. 36:9, 10; 42:1, 2; 65:10-14), was at that time also a classic symbol of salvation (Isa. 12:3; 44:3; 55:1-3). God describes Himself as 'a Fountain of living water' Jer. 2:13; 17:13.

[10] The social status of a woman depended to a large extent upon the man. A woman could not do certain things without the consent of her husband (if married) or of her father (if single). Among such things were asking for a divorce, making a pledge, or making any decision which would compromise her religious life (Num. 30:4-16). Wives and daughters were listed as part of the wealth of the husband, along with houses, lands, servants, etc. Daughters could be sold as slaves in some cases (Exod. 21:7-11), but they could not be purchased for prostitution (Lev. 19:29). Wives and daughters inherited from their husband or father only if there were no male heirs (the only known exception was that of the daughters of Job (Job 42:15), but Job was not an Israelite!

[11] Common law permitted the woman to be married only three times. Any further attempt at marriage was considered illegal (*Niddah* 64a; *Yebamoth* 64b).

[12] In reality, all we know about this woman's private life is mere conjecture. Here five husbands could have been lawfully married to her and either died or been divorced. Jesus refers to an irregular situation only in regard to the sixth.

[13] Between the years 108 and 129BC the temple on Mt. Gerizim was destroyed by John Hyrcanus but the ritual sacrifices continued there.

[14] Only men could hold religious office. The law rejected foreigners and bastards (Deut. 23:1, 2), the deformed and disabled (Lev. 21:16-24), the diseased (Lev. 22:1-9), the sexually deficient (Deut. 23:1). All those exclusions would have no part in the new covenant (Isa. 56:3-8; Gal. 3:27-29).

[15] The worship of God in spirit and in truth is a question of attitude and sincerity rather than strict orthodoxy. God bears in mind the knowledge available to each person. Faithfulness to conscience and to the revelations received is more important than forms or methods of worship. See Rom. 2:12-16.

[16] According to Deut. 18:15-18, the Samaritans awaited the coming of a messianic prophet 'like Moses' called Ta'eb (he who is to come).

[17] John 4:27-42 tells how, because of that unnamed woman, Jesus began His ministry evangelizing Samaria. The Samaritan was, then, the first Christian missionary in recorded history.

At the beach

Squalls of rain whip the sides of the cliff and angry waves smash against the rocks. Dug-out tombs along the edge of the precipice grin sinisterly in the white lightning of the stormy night.

The man shakes with cold. He has managed to break his chains but only by wounding himself. Now in that pit, that common grave which serves as his refuge, he feels as never before the pain of his loneliness.

He cannot think clearly any more, but he is aware that he is not in control of himself. No longer possessed only by despair or insanity, he is possessed by demons.

Even his loved ones have abandoned him. Frightened and propelled by the townsmen, they brought him to the graveyard and chained him there, not to protect him but to be protected from him.[1] He is condemned to this life, condemned to this death — forever.

He trembles in the crashing tempest. But the storm in his soul, much greater than the storm that blows around him, is destroying him, and he knows it.

A convulsive scream from one of his unfortunate companions breaks into the silence of his thoughts and wrenches him back to dismal reality.[2]

'That is I. I am just like him. I am nothing more than a shred of humanity who evokes not pity but revulsion and fear.'

He falls to the ground, sobbing. The early-morning chill wraps around his naked body. The open sores from his chains burn. And while he lies on the ground in despair, his crazy companion stands above him, laughing with satanic glee. This unfortunate wretch mirrors his plight. This graveyard is his world. Will death never come to rescue him? Must another day dawn upon his agony?

It has stopped raining. The wind has died down and the clouds have parted. On the lake below, the last rays of moonlight dance across the silent sea.[3] Far away the Gerasene sees the silhouette of a nearing ship. He feels a strange longing for peace pass over him. Without knowing how or why, he finds himself descending the cliff to the shore, to an encounter.

The boat comes aground. A young man, who keeps eye-contact with him, smiles and leaps ashore, followed slowly by a group of frightened young fishermen. The man comes towards him. The demoniac feels his heart turn somersault. This man may be Jesus. He has heard about Jesus and His strange powers.

Gathering his last bit of strength, in an impulsive gesture which he hardly understands, the demoniac runs towards the man and falls face down at His feet.[4]

The demoniac hears voices of alarm and retreating steps, followed by an expectant silence. Certain that his behaviour has frightened away the visitor and that he has lost his only chance, he dares not lift his gaze from the ground. But as he slowly rises, his eyes fall upon the resolute features of Jesus, bronzed from the sun and wind. Jesus is still there!

And without wanting to, the demoniac screams uncontrollably: '"What do you want with me, Jesus, Son of the Most High God? I beg you, don't torture me!"'[5]

But the One who has faced the storm on the Sea of Galilee and who has battled Satan in person so many times does not fear this demon-possessed man. The One who created man in His own image does not take even one step back at the sight of one so far removed from the image of God. Jesus ignores the Satanic darkness surrounding the man. He treats him simply as a suffering soul. Beyond the uncontrolled words, behind the gestures of rejection, Jesus hears a cry for help. He hears, 'Help me!' while the man cries, 'Leave me in peace!'

Jesus wants to enter into a personal relationship with the sick man and looks for his friendship.

'"What is your name?"'[6]

The stranger's voice penetrates as a ray of hope in the tired mind of the Gerasene, who seems to understand vaguely that he is in the presence of Someone who can free him.[7]

But when he tries to give his name, the devils answer with a sinister roar: 'My name is Legion; for we are many.'

Why this strange answer? In that society, knowing someone's name meant having, in some form, access to that person. For that reason it was believed to be necessary to name the demon when trying to cast him out in exorcist rites.[8] The spirits' unwillingness to give their individual names may be seen as presumptuous boasting, designed to impede the exorcism. Or perhaps the possessed man was confessing to the enormity and the impossibility of identifying all the demons by name.

It is also worth mentioning that at that time Palestine was occupied by Roman legions. The word 'legion' had come to mean total subjugation to a foreign power whose overwhelming superiority made it invincible. It describes better than any other the plight of the Gerasene.

In any case, Jesus does not need the man's name in order to understand his need. Nor does Jesus classify the man by his devil-possession. This is a mere circumstance and does not change his value before God. Jesus sees that, when liberated, this man will change totally.

God does not evaluate us by what we are now, but by what we can become. He knows that the powers now dominating us are, in the end, alien to us. He knows that if we choose to let them go they will become nothing more than a foggy memory of our past existence.

In spite of what we have been taught, we do not need to be 'good' in order to receive His grace. He accepts us as we are. But He loves us too much to leave us in our present condition. His eyes see beyond our painful present to a victorious future. And so He comes to lift us from the quagmire. He extends to us His outstretched hand and His grace so that we can become 'good'.[9]

God's way is so different from ours that it is difficult for us to believe that He accepts us in spite of our mistakes; and that we are valuable to Him, not for what we do or for who we are but for what we can become through His power. God is the One 'Who gives life to the dead and calls things that are not as though they were.'[10]

Jesus teaches that independently of our behaviour God treats us not according to our deserts but our needs. For this reason He does not always give us what we ask, but what is best for us.

In the case of the Gerasene, Jesus knew that although the demoniac did not ask for it, he wanted to be liberated. And so, with a calm voice full of authority, Jesus ordered the legion: '"Come out of this man, you evil spirit!"'[11]

Demon possession in biblical times was complex. The problem was that it was difficult to determine at which point some really became demon-possessed. The lack of sufficient medical knowledge placed any inexplicable symptom of epilepsy or malaria among those of demon-possession.[12]

Although demon-possessed people like the man in our story are not common sights today, demon possession in one form or another is more prevalent among us than we care to admit.[13]

Today it is just as easy, if not more so, to be a victim of spirits as devastating as alcoholism, violence, envy, avarice, lust, injustice, or indifference. There are legions of them. These filthy spirits,[14] in a way less pompous and more subtle, can shackle and drag us down to the edge of despair. They may not control in legions, but they are too numerous to be ignored. They are infernal demons, and they seek to destroy us by throwing us into the gutters or leaving us to drift between the precipices and graveyards of our modern Gerasa.

We all know what it means to be 'possessed' by evil. We have all felt the whip of the diabolical oppressor who is always lying in wait, ready to defeat us on every front. In a moment of clarity between battles, relapses, and disappointments we, too, dare to hope.

In the silent moments when we dare to look within, we feel as did the Gerasene, naked and helpless. It is so hard to admit that, more than victims, we are accomplices of the tyrant. It is so painful to admit our failures. We would like to free ourselves. We would like victory without a mediator. We would like to have light without the sun. Yet, in the end, we must admit that we are as helpless as the Gerasene.

But his story brings us hope. An Eternal Advocate has been following our battles, suffering our sorrows, waiting for us to admit our need for help. He has come searching for us in our own rugged coastline graveyard. Although we may be as clumsy or unsteady in our cry for help as the Gerasene, his story proves to us that there is no hopeless situation for the one who accepts God's help.

Jesus says: '"Come to me, all whose work is hard, whose load is heavy; and I will give you relief.[15] Whoever comes to me I will never drive away."'[16]

The moment in which we realize that we are enslaved by certain things, the moment in which we admit that we love our slavery, is the moment when we can be sure that the Advocate is trying to break into our lives to lead us to freedom in Him. We can be sure that He will lead us to freedom because where He is oppression cannot exist.

Gerasa, a semi-pagan land, was plagued by demons. Jesus knew that, and instead of giving a theological discourse on demonology or antidemonology, He simply chose to demonstrate God's power over the demons. He was not concerned with the nature or power of demons. He was interested in freeing men from them. Jesus reached out to that demon-possessed man and performed a miracle so that all in Gerasa might see what He could accomplish in their own lives.

The story continues with the Gerasene dressed and calmly seated at the feet of his new Teacher, listening to His words.[17]

This great change does not go unnoticed. The story tells us that on the rocky shelf which overhung the beach, was a herd of pigs. Although to the Jews the animals were unclean, some country folk took advantage of the pagan demand for meat and bred and sold pigs. The devil immediately saw his opportunity to incite hostility towards Jesus in the region. So the legion had the diabolical idea to possess the pigs and throw them into the sea.[18]

The story does not tell us why Jesus allowed such an economically disastrous ending. Perhaps He wanted to take advantage of that spectacular plunge to demonstrate that, although there is a 'dozing pig' in each of us,[19] in God's eyes we are of more value than any other considerations, even economic ones. Jesus puts things into their rightful place:

the Gerasene with peace in his heart and the demon-possessed pigs.[20]

But this action conflicts with the economic interests of the pig herders. Upset by their losses they do not ask Jesus to heal their sick. Rather, they beg Him to leave.[21] Their revenue interests them more than their souls.

It is a common human reaction. When Divine power begins to transform our lives, those around us notice. But not everyone reacts supportively. The pig herders of the world are not interested in our personal well-being.

When a drug addict or an alcoholic defeats his dependency, his family rejoices. But his suppliers and his old friends tempt him with a fix or a drink.

Unfortunately, it is a lucrative business providing grazing for those human beings who by their attitudes lower themselves, not to the level of animals, but of subhumans. Think of the huge business behind drugs, pornography, or arms trafficking!

We all have to choose between being controlled by the Spirit or by opportunists and extortionists.

The text concludes by saying that, as Jesus embarks to continue His journey, the Gerasene begs to be allowed to go with Him.[22]

We all prefer to lean on someone else rather than face the cruel reality that surrounds us. But Jesus teaches a life-style of brotherhood. And so with all the love in the world, Jesus refuses the Gerasene's request. Instead, He gives him a mission: '"Go home to your family and tell them how much the Lord has done for you, and how he has had mercy on you."'[23]

Jesus' words awaken within the Gerasene's heart a new instinct of brotherhood. The man decides to return home to share with his family his marvellous encounter with Jesus. With new strength surging through his body, he begins to run so as not to look backwards, so as not to cry, so as not to shout his joy. Now he is a free man. A new day has dawned and has chased away his stormy night.

In the same way that Jesus saw more than a madman that day in Gerasa, so He can see beyond our despair. He sees the enormous potential that is within each of us. Jesus crossed Lake Galilee in search of the Gerasene, and He is searching for us as well.

The story of the Gerasene proves that there is no hopeless situation for one who accepts God's offer. The frightening, demon-possessed Gerasene was converted into the first missionary of Decapolis. Nobody can predict what we will become once God's power rescues us from our despair.

---

[1]Mark 5:1-5. Demon-possessed people were kept in places believed to be inhabited by the devil. Such places included cemeteries, city ruins (*Berakoth* 3a b), marshes and miry places, swamps, wild and savage places, dungheaps, latrines (*Berakoth* 62 a), and forests (*Sanhedrin* 44 a).

Luke 8:26, 27, 29 states that the man in question was city-bred. The graves of that period were cavelike holes dug horizontally into the rock. Such graves, occupied and unoccupied alike, often served as places of refuge for lepers, the insane, demon-possessed and others rejected by society who stayed in the chambers designed for the dead. Those were the types of graves referred to in almost all New Testament texts. (See John 20:5, 6; Mark 15:46; Matt. 27:66.)

[2]Mark and Luke (not disciples) only mention one demoniac. But Matthew, without doubt an eyewitness to the events, states that there were two men. (Matt. 8:28-34.)

[3]The three gospels which describe this incident place it on the morning after the storm on the Sea of Galilee (Matt. 8:18, 23-27; Mark 4:35-41; Luke 8:22-25). Gerasa was a small town located a little more than six miles to the south of the mouth of the Jordan along the north-east coast of the Sea of Galilee.

[4]Mark 5:6.

[5]Mark 5:7; Luke 8:28, NIV.

[6]Mark 5:9; Luke 8:30, NIV.

[7]*The Desire of Ages*, pages 337, 338.

[8]There is a collection of traditional personalized conjurations and spells such as: 'I found the demon Bar Shirika Panda. In the leek patch I conquered him. With an ass's jawbone I struck him. . . .' (*Shabbath* 67 a) (*'Abodah Zarah* 30 b). Another one goes like this: 'Dismembered, destroyed, cursed and exiled will you be, son of mud, son of filth, son of dust, Shamgaz, Mengaz or Istemaah' (*Shabbath* 67 a). One form of exorcising a demon, provided its name was known, went like this: 'Be careful, Shabriri, Briri, Riri, Iri, Ri, i' (*Pesahim* 112 a). The influence of the devil was reduced little by little as the name was reduced until it fully disappeared.

[9]See *Steps to Christ*, The Stanborough Press Ltd., page 31.

[10]Rom. 4:17, NIV.

[11]Mark 5:8, NIV.

[12]Demon possession was generally considered a direct result of trans-

42 AT THE BEACH

gressing one of the Divine laws. (Sotah 3 a). About the difficulty of distinguishing between possession and illness, see Matt. 17:14-18, a text where the patient is treated indiscriminately as sick, insane, and demon-possessed.

[13] In order to convince ourselves that the demon does, indeed, 'possess' us, we need only to take a look around us (doesn't Jean Paul Sartre say in *Huis Clos*, that 'hell is found in those around us'?) or look at ourselves in the mirror. . . .

[14] 'Filthy', in biblical language, signifies 'contaminated' and 'contaminating' both at the same time.

[15] Matt. 11:28, NEB.

[16] John 6:37, NIV.

[17] Mark 5:15; Luke 8:35.

[18] Mark 5:11-13; Luke 8:31-34. It was believed that evil spirits attacked animals as often or more than they did people. Rabies in dogs was believed to be demon-possession (Yoma 83 b).

[19] Phrase attributed to Charles Monselet (*Larousse des citations Francaises*, Paris, 1976, page 673).

[20] I owe this idea to my exceptional student and dear friend, Juan Ramon Junqueras.

[21] Mark 5:14-17; Luke 8:35-37.

[22] Mark 5:18; Luke 8:38.

[23] Mark 5:19, 20, NIV; Luke 8:39.

In the courtyard

Here on the edge of town near the east gate,[1] she lies huddled, alone. They have thrown her down among the temple-building supplies which lie scattered about. Half-naked and panting like a trapped animal, she watches her betrayers close in around her. She sees a circle of accusing fingers and cruel smiles.

Why had they dragged her from her bed to throw her down here on the cold pavement of the temple courtyard? Why have her friends betrayed her? Why have they picked up stones?

A voice masked with offended righteousness screams out so all can hear: 'This woman was caught in the act of adultery. In the law, Moses commanded us to stone such women.[2] Now what do you say?'[3]

The words fall like a whiplash and the woman flinches. The death sentence does not surprise her so much. But she is amazed at the identity of the one who is demanding it.

Her head sinks down upon the stones. So she will die here today as a common sinner. What an absurd irony her life has been! She looked for liberty and found slavery. She needed love and received lust. She wanted friends and found only cruel executioners. She wanted, more than anything else, happiness; but, instead, had brought on her own destruction.

Jesus knows what her life has been. He knows that everything began with that crazy, youthful rebelliousness when she had still believed in her dreams. Naïvely, like so many young people, she had chased after the superficial attraction of the forbidden. In order to escape the dissatisfaction and mediocrity of life, she had buried herself in new pleasures and new sensations. But they did not last. And now, at a time which could have been her end, she has reaped sadness, shame, and loneliness.

She lies motionless and resigned, awaiting her fate. But then she sees the young teacher, Jesus of Nazareth. She has heard Him preach love and forgiveness. Will He have compassion on her today?

Of the entire crazed pack, He alone does not look at her. All the respect in the world hides behind those averted eyes. He stares at the ground as if He has not heard the accusations.

But He has heard the cry of the woman's heart. He hears her regrets over a wasted life. He hears her shame at having given in to the whims of men who could never love her back. He understands her bitterness at having been used by those who claimed to care for her. He sees the open sores of so much rejection and scorn. He knows her failures.

More importantly, however, He sees her desire to be pure. He knows that no one has given her the opportunity to do right. He knows that she has been pushed down by others and left to bear the guilt alone.

Jesus reads more than the woman's heart. He also sees beyond the righteous indignation of her accusers. Although Moses allowed stoning, the more usual punishment was divorce. By ignoring the custom of the day and reverting to a harsher legal sentence, these men expose their true motives. Morality does not bring them here. They do not respect the Law, nor do they love virtue. They are merely using this woman as bait. Jesus is their target. He defends sinners in His teachings and His enemies choose to present Him with a real case in order to trap Him.

If the young preacher maintains His doctrine of mercy and understanding, they can easily accuse Him of preaching a subversive message. By refusing to uphold the sentence handed down by Moses, He will make flagrantly clear His rejection of the sacred Scriptures. They can accuse Him of sacrilege and wickedness, not only before the religious authorities, but also before the public.[4]

If, by some remote chance, He upholds the sentence established by the Law, the consequences will be even worse. He will clearly contradict His own teachings of compassion and forgiveness. He will, in this way, lose all credibility. As a final indignity they can immediately drag Him before the

Sanhedrin and the Roman authorities for pronouncing a death sentence without authority.[5]

They have laid the trap well, and Jesus weighs His alternatives. If He refuses to pronounce judgement He will be accused of being a coward. He quickly realizes, however, that He can enter into the judicial conflict and use the Law to defeat them.

According to the penal code of the day, there are two irregularities which His enemies have overlooked and which He can use in His favour. Firstly, only the cheated husband has the power to accuse his wife of infidelity.[6] Secondly, the law demands that both the adulteress and her lover be stoned together.[7] Either of these would be reason enough to dismiss the case and prove the incompetence and corruption of the accusers, thus placing them in a very embarrassing position.

Jesus does not choose this easy option. He moves the issue to a higher sphere. Instead of defending a principle He chooses to defend a person. Since the offended husband is not present, no one has any legal right to accuse the woman. This allows Him to address the moral issue.

By accusing the woman, the Pharisees place themselves in a position of moral superiority. Jesus knows the depth of their hypocrisy.

The law dictated that in a stoning the witnesses should first apply the punishment, followed by others in the crowd. However, there was a condition attached. A person suspected of committing a similar offence could not be a participating agent.[8]

Jesus addressed the most distinguished ones: '"If any one of you is without sin, let him be the first to throw a stone at her."'[9] He then bends to the ground and begins to write.

A heavy silence falls. The woman, who has shrunk back, expecting the first stone, awaits her fate, wishing the torture would end. Tension hangs thick in the air.

Irritated by Jesus' silence, some of the men draw near. What they see makes them drop their stones. There, for all to see, Jesus has scratched in the dust the deeds which prove them to be as guilty as the woman, if not more so.[10]

They tremble with rage and shame. One by one they all

disappear into the shadows, some because of what has been revealed and others for fear of what could still be revealed. They leave the accused alone with her judge.

Jesus does not usurp the authority of the Law. He does not involve Himself in any legal controversy. With a few words scratched in dust, Jesus curbs the wicked plans of the Pharisees and saves a woman's life.

When at last Jesus straightens up, He sees the woman gazing up at Him with wonder in her eyes. He extends His hand, helping her to rise, and with a smile creasing His lips He says: 'Woman, where are they? Has no one condemned you?'

She looks about her, blinded by the morning light. She sees only stones upon the deserted pavement of the courtyard.[11] Incredulous, she responds: 'No one, Sir.'

'Neither do I condemn you. Go now and change direction. Leave your life of sin.'[12]

Accustomed to being treated by men as an object to be discarded after use, and knowing as she did the hatred and jealousy of other women, the 'Go now' sounded all too familiar. The 'Leave your life of sin' was also something she had heard a hundred times, in a hundred different ways, from the continual reproaches of her family to the sermons of the priests. But 'Neither do I condemn you'? That she had never heard before. Nobody had ever spoken to her in that tone of voice. Jesus was the first person who did not judge her, who did not lust after her, who did not humiliate her. This man pitied her for her mistakes. He understood her plight and believed in her repentance. He helped her to accept God's forgiveness. He saw her potential and helped her to believe that she really did have a future.

In that instant she knew that she had begun a new life. Wrapped in the radiant whiteness of the courtyard, she felt transformed, purified, at peace with God. She felt happy at last.

The woman lingered, knowing that though she had to go, she would return soon and then would never leave the presence of this teacher who had given her back her dignity and her honour.

We, too, linger in His presence, wishing for His acceptance. Jesus knows that we need more love than we deserve. He understands our mistakes. He extends His hand to us and with love and absolute respect, He says to us, 'I know that all you can see is failure. But I see treasures lying dormant in your hearts. Come, leave the pain behind. I offer you a future of acceptance and love.'

Story based on John 8:2-11.

[1] The Temple in Jerusalem was built by Herod the Great and was begun in the year 19BC (*Ant.* 15:2, 1). It was not completed until the years AD62-64 by the procurator Albinus, just before it was destroyed by the Romans. It consisted of the sanctuary, along with a series of terraced buildings. The scene of the story takes place in an open area called the 'outer courtyard' or the 'Court of the Gentiles'. It was extensive and served as the public plaza. The 'courtyard' was the meeting place of Jerusalem. Jews and pagans alike went there to conduct business. It was enclosed by covered colonnades, sometimes referred to as porches, in which the people used to take walks. The doctors of the Law, surrounded by their disciples, sat there to teach (Matt. 26:55). It was also where animals were sold for sacrifices (Mark 11:15), and money was exchanged for the offerings since the temple accepted only its own currency.

[2] Among the sins which could be punished by stoning were blasphemy and adultery. Cf. Lev. 24:14; Deut. 17:2-5; 2 Chr. 24:20-22; *Sanhedrin* 7, 1, 4.

[3] John 8:4, 5. cf Lev. 20:10.

[4] The preaching that love was superior to the Law was, without doubt, the most disturbing part of Jesus' message, cf. Matt. 5:38-48, especially since it transcended all the demands of the Torah.

[5] The Sanhedrin met in the temple twice a week, led by the high priest. They had the power to create laws; they had their own police force; and they could sentence someone to death, although, in the time of Jesus, they were not allowed to apply the death penalty. They determined the liturgic calendar and regulated the religious life. (Josephus, *Ant.* 2:138 of Acts 5:21.)

[6] The text doesn't say that the husband was the accuser. Rather, it refers to a group of scribes and Pharisees (John 8:3). In Jesus' time the normal punishment for adultery was divorce, not stoning (Deut. 22:19, 29. *Kethuboth* 3, 5.)

[7] The impartiality of the sentence, which made no discrimination between the woman and the man guilty of adultery, is clear in biblical law (cf. Deut. 22:22-24; Lev. 20:10.)

[8] Deut. 17:7. The right of the participation of the witnesses *was* backed by common law. (*b Sotah* 47 b.)

[9] John 8:7, NIV.

[10] *The Desire of Ages*, page 461.

[11] A stoning could take place only outside the city. (Lev. 24:14; 2 Chr.

24:20-22; Matt. 21:35.) The fact that the accusers came carrying rocks makes sense when one realizes that the East Gate of the Outer Courtyard (called Solomon's Gate, John 10:23; Acts 3:11; 5:12) opens directly on the Kidron river. The city ends there; and, even today, next to the temple wall there is only a cemetery. If one keeps in mind the fact that at that time the temple had been under construction for forty-six years (John 2:20), it could be supposed that they could have picked the stones from among the building supplies which were lying about.

[12]In the New Testament there are several Greek terms from which we translate 'sin'. The most common are: *adikia* (twenty-two times), 'iniquity', which means a crime against the law; *parabasis* (fourteen times), 'transgression', meaning a violation of God's Divine Law; but most times (296 to be exact) the word used is *hamartia*. This comes from the verb *hamartano* (used in John 8:11) and means 'to aim badly' as in sports (archery, the javelin and discus throw), in hunting, or in war (Homer, *Iliad* 5:287; Aeschylus, *Fragmenta* 179). It can also mean 'to detour' or 'to take a wrong turn' (Aristophanes, *Plutus* 961). Finally, it can mean 'to err' or 'to commit a mistake' or 'to fail to reach the objective' (Sophocles, *Philoctetes* 231) or to 'miss the mark or overshoot it' (Homer, *Iliad* 11:522). The word *hamartia* really means to 'make a mistake' either out of clumsiness or ignorance (Plato, *Leges* 759).

The Hebrew meaning for sin (*het* or *avon*) refers to a break in the relationship between God and man. So sin is, therefore, to be unfaithful to the covenant, to betray the love of God, to separate oneself from communion with God.

At the foot of the mountain

He has tried all the remedies, medicines, treatments, diets and spells[1] but his son's condition does not improve. He has consulted all the doctors and tried all the potions they have to offer. They have taken his money and his hope. Just as any father whose child is sick, he will do everything, give anything, to find a cure.

That first terrible attack is repeated day after day. His little boy twists and thrashes about on the floor, spitting foam and grinding his teeth until he finally goes rigid and then limp.[2] Each time death draws nearer. The father knows there is not much time left for his son. He knows it, yet he cannot cry. The unending tragedy weighs upon him so heavily that he no longer knows how to cry. Sealed in a vacuum of pain and despair, he can hardly feel anything any more. Can this quiet desperation be called living?

No. There must be something more. He continues to grasp at any chance, at any suggestion; because as long as he continues to search for and try any cure available, he can persuade himself that he is delaying the final crisis.

He is the father of the deaf mute. This is what his neighbours call him. Actually, no one knows for sure what is wrong with the child, and the diagnoses range from lunacy to demon possession.[3] All anyone knows is that it is hopeless. He has tried everything but nothing helps, not even praying. His relatives want him to give up.

'What are you going to do? There is no remedy. You must resign yourself to the fact that this is your destiny.'

But he continues to rebel against the idea that he must accept this unbearable situation. He cannot give up until the end. Since he has nothing more to lose, he must continue to look for a solution. If there is an answer, he must find it. Life cannot be so cruel. He continues to fight . . . against the helplessness of men and the silence of God.

Alone, afraid, and seemingly abandoned in our fight we know that God is love, and we struggle to understand how He can allow such evil and suffering to engulf us. We need faith, but we do not know, any more, what it means to believe.

We, too, cry out against God's silence. It may be cancer or some other life-threatening disease. It may be a natural disaster such as a hurricane or an earthquake; or it may be a human disaster such as homelessness, substance abuse, or war. Whatever it is, it mercilessly erodes our security and our sanity, and undermines our beliefs.

The Bible never describes faith in terms of privilege but of relationship. To believe in God is to live in a relationship with Him. This relationship can be described as a journey of discovery or exploration. It is difficult and requires commitment. It is easy to lose one's way, and one may be required to risk life itself. Hoping — and losing hope — in the end we find the unexpected reward just when all seems lost.

We give the word 'faith' a completely religious meaning; but in the biblical languages there is not a specific word for religious faith. The word translated 'faith' means confidence placed in someone because we feel that person is worthy of it. The dictionary defines faith as 'Confidence, reliance, trust (in the ability, goodness, etc. of a person; in the efficacy or worth of a thing; or in the truth of a statement or doctrine).'[4] The Gospel says that 'faith gives substance to our hopes, and makes us certain of realities we do not see'. Other versions say that it means 'putting our full confidence in the things we hope for, . . . (and) being certain of things we cannot see.'[5] Faith is made up more of confidence than belief, more of intuition than conviction, more of discipleship than certainty. Perhaps 'discipleship' is the proper word.[6] It indicates a commitment and a turning towards something or someone without necessarily requiring total understanding. It is possible to believe in someone without understanding him completely.

The success of the trip of faith depends completely upon our willingness to follow our Guide through all weathers and in all circumstances. We need not have the full facts. We can be on God's side without comprehending His silence.

This adventure is a constant battle against the limitations

of the human condition, but the adventurer has the certainty that victory is assured. In this pact, God does not guarantee to free us from all danger, but He does promise to give us the strength necessary to overcome it.

The father of the deaf mute does not understand God's silence, but he does not give in to despair. He continues to search and his search leads him to the foot of the mountain and to Jesus.

But Jesus is not here and the disciples can do nothing.[7] When Jesus finally arrives, the father is so discouraged that he does not even ask Jesus to heal his son. He merely recites, as he has done so many times to so many others, his son's symptoms. Almost as an afterthought, he adds: 'Sir, if it is at all possible for you, take pity on us and help us.'

Jesus trembles before this shameful spectacle. The child rolls on the ground in pain and his father, unable to take any more, slumps down nearby with his head in his hands. Meanwhile, Jesus' disciples stand a short way off, theorizing with a group of religious teachers about the situation.

'Oh, unbelieving generation, how long will I stay with you? How long will I put up with you?'

Jesus' indignation against 'this unbelieving generation'[8] was directed not at the father but at His own disciples. He did not rebuke them because they had failed to cure the child but because they had tried to do it in their own power. Their lack of a living experience with God — that is, their lack of faith — had led them to act as if their 'professional' proximity to Jesus was enough to convert them into His executive officers and agents (sometimes, secret agents) of His power.

Crouching down to protect the convulsing body of the child with His arms, Jesus answers the father: 'Is it possible? Everything is possible for him who believes.'[9]

With this simple proclamation, Jesus invites the father to trust in God the way He, Himself, does. Miracles are divine gifts, and only our trust in divine power can lead to divine intervention.

The tormented father raises his head at Jesus' words, but he does not understand. He feels so beaten, so desperate. Is it possible that belief alone can end this nightmare? Can his faith as a father save his son? Moved by his grief, he jumps up and cries: 'I believe!'

Yet he is too sincere to try to fool Jesus, and he adds: 'Lord, I would like to believe, but there is something inside me that is forcing me to doubt. On the one hand, I believe that God can do anything, but, on the other hand, there's a voice inside telling me that it cannot be true. Weigh my unbelief, take into account my desire to believe. Help me even though I am not sure that you are going to heal my son.'[10]

How many times, like this father, are we so filled with doubts that we are unsure as to whether we believe or not? Have we not all asked God, at some time or other, to help us believe?

And yet, this moment when we feel defeated, this final confession of helplessness in which we recognize our absolute inability even to hope, is all that is needed. This final effort to give ourselves entirely to God is the necessary faith which makes everything possible.

Some say that they cannot believe because faith is a gift which God gives only to a few. But this line of reasoning cannot be valid. The fact that faith is a gift from God does not justify the disbelief of anyone. Life is also a gift. The idea that God arbitrarily hands out faith to whom He chooses is not biblical. The Bible clearly says: 'God has no favourites,'[11] and speaks of 'the measure of faith that God has dealt to each of you'.[12] The amount can vary in the same way that lung capacity varies or mental abilities are different; but everyone has the possibility of perceiving God.

Faith is not just a beautiful and mystical ideal. Faith is what enables us, when we face the horrors of evil and suffering, to search for a solution where there apparently is none. Faith is what helps us fight to the end of our strength. Faith led the father of the deaf mute to the foot of the mountain and to this encounter with Jesus. Can it be that God does not ask us for more than the sincere desire to believe?

The father of the deaf mute trusts Jesus because intuitively he feels that Jesus is on his side. This faith which functions without demonstrations and which grasps without seeing, this 'Godly instinct' is all that is needed. The father needs it, not so much so that his son can be cured, but simply to be able to fight, to endure, and to step beyond the reality of his life, even if his son is not cured.

God decides to perform a miracle and, in that very moment, the deaf mute is healed. But this happened only when his father was willing to accept God's divine plan — on trust; not knowing what it was — without demanding anything.

Suffering is so difficult to endure if we depend on our own resources. Only if we believe can we look at suffering head-on without closing our eyes, without ignoring the horror of it, without resigning ourselves to it, and without rebelling against the apparent silence of God.

The believer knows that God is near and that He came to bear our pain by becoming a man. *True faith is absolute confidence in the fact that God is on our side.* We can have this confidence because Jesus has shared our pain and has conquered it. He is the guarantor of life. His miracles are no more than the security deposit of the truthfulness of His promises and of His final triumph.

To believe is to trust in the only Being capable of saving us from ourselves and of giving sense and order to our lives. It means saying 'yes' to Someone who not only accepts us without looking at our past, but who accompanies us, transforming our present, and guiding us to a brighter future.

Believing, like living, is passionate. It is an adventure full of risk and of the unforeseen. It is also full of enormous satisfaction. Believing, like loving, means to commit oneself and to decide to share the most intimate part of self with Someone. It means uniting with Him without reservations. Knowing that He loves us, it means loving Him in return.

Since faith is commitment, it is not found by chance the way we find a coin on the street. Nor is it lost as a handbag might be. It cannot be kept in a long-term savings account in a bank. It is a living relationship which will either grow and develop or wither and die.

The same way that a friendship or a love relationship cannot survive merely on formal visits or forced conversations, the relationship with God, our faith in Him, will die from starvation if we limit it to obligatory meetings and formal occasions.

Establishing a solid relationship takes years; but sometimes one moment of impatience can end it all. Perhaps for this reason, in the world in which we live where no one has time for others and where patience is so scarce, there are fewer and fewer believers. Although there are many substitute faiths, our post-Christian world is losing faith itself, and at such a pace that Jesus asked if, at His return, there would be any of the faithful left on the earth.[13]

Unfortunately, part of the responsibility for this situation must lie with some who call themselves Christians.

One university student wrote to me, asking: 'How can I accept within the same church Bishop X who supports the guerillas in Central America and Bishop Y who dies in condemning them? One supports the dominating class and the other has died to liberate those who are oppressed by them. One will vindicate the aggressor while the other will liberate the victorious. How can the exploiter and the exploited worship together, then return to their respective roles during the week? Such a situation undermines my faith and encourages me to leave the Church.'

It is, unfortunately, all too common to see believers carry their treasure of faith in a container so worldly and mundane that it devalues the contents.[14] It hurts to think that someone can leave the Church, forget his religion and lose his faith because his sense of rightness has been offended by the conduct of some who call themselves Christians. But it is even more painful that some who search for God abandon that search because they are repelled by His self-appointed representatives.

In his letters to Timothy, Paul lists the reasons for this crisis of faith. The first is the perversion of the divine teachings: 'In later times some will abandon the faith and follow deceiving spirits and things taught by demons.'[15] Only the discovery of the divine revelation can resolve the confusion provoked by the proliferation of strange beliefs.

The second reason has to do with 'the opposing ideas of what is falsely called knowledge, which some have professed and in so doing have wandered from the faith.'[16] There are theories which present certain materialistic arguments as the only valid ones to explain the mysteries of origin and the meaning of life. These theories presuppose that the idea of God belongs to an age of prelogical thinking which has been superseded by the culture scholarship of today. An impartial study of the difference between hypothesis and proven fact would place the question upon a much more scientific basis, thus allowing for the possibility of other explanations.

The third reason for losing the faith, according to Paul, is the secularization of a materialistic society: 'People who want to get rich fall into temptation and a trap and into many foolish and harmful desires that plunge men into ruin and destruction. For the love of money is a root of all kinds of evil. Some people, eager for money, have wandered from the faith and pierced themselves with many griefs.'[17] In a realistic way, the Bible warns against the dangers of putting earthly possessions first. ''''Man does not live on bread alone.''''[18] To close oneself to the spiritual dimension of life leads to indisputable mutilation.

We could discuss many more factors which tend to separate us from our faith. But we wouldn't find any that was independent of ourselves, thus affording sufficient reason to justify breaking with God.

Fortunately, faith can be discovered and cultivated in the simplest way. When God comes out to meet us, we need only to open ourselves to His influence, even if it is just to say, 'Help me to believe.' This, in itself, is an act of faith. Although we do not experience any special happening, each longing to discover a purpose in life, each desire to experience the ideal, each wish to do something good for someone, is an indication of our responding to the call of faith.

By developing our relationship with God and by sharing it with those around us — because God's love is found in our fellow man — our faith grows and our life is enriched. Then, even the day-to-day difficulties will help unite us to Him more and more. Then we will have discovered that, although He does not always keep the storm away from the door, He is always there to help us fight against it. We will know that if He doesn't always protect the boat, He can always protect the sailor.

Because of Jesus, we can see beyond the suffering and death and glimpse eternity when good will finally triumph. We know that all human explanations of evil are futile and that only through resistance to the devil will brotherhood and hope prevail. Believing, although it does not resolve the horror of evil, enables us to live on in the knowledge of its final eradication. There is no magic formula for believing, for solving our conflicts, for coping with grief. There is the power to fight against all the odds, the evil which seeks to separate us from the One who loves us, and the One we love.

From this perspective, the opposite of believing isn't doubting — but rejecting. For this reason the worst sin, and the one which Jesus condemns most severely, is indifference and scorn.[19]

When, later, the disciples asked Him why they had been unable to cure the child, Jesus told them that it was possible to find certain solutions only through 'prayer and fasting',[20] which means depending totally upon God.

And so, at the end of the story, Jesus says to His disciples: 'If you had faith like a mustard seed, you could move mountains.'[21]

With these words He reminds them that the essential thing is their relationship with God: that although in the beginning it is very weak, it remains alive. If we allow the relationship to take root, it will become, as in the parable, a power to remove our mountains of doubt.

If our relationship with God is our first priority, if like the father of the deaf mute we bring to Him our heavy burdens, we can be sure that He will help us to carry them. Our faith will continue to flourish and grow. And that, in the times in which we live, does not cease to be a miracle.

---

[1] We know of a number of cures which were used for various illnesses. Josephus relates one of the classic chants: 'Place a ring which had the stamp of the roots prescribed by Solomon close to the nose of the demon-possessed so that he could smell it; and when the man fell to the floor, order the devil not to return in the name of Solomon and recite the incantation which Solomon wrote.' (*Ant.* 8:45, 49.) Another example of a possible treatment is the following: 'Sit the patient in an intersection. When you see the first ant which is carrying a burden, kill it and place it in a copper tube, plug it with lead and stamp it with sixty stamps. Shake it from one side to another, shouting, "Your weight be on me and my weight on you."' (*Shabbath* 46 b). For the weaker fevers (associated with devil possession) the following was prescribed: 'Take seven splinters from seven palm trees, seven chips from seven beams, seven nails from seven bridges, seven pieces of ash from seven ovens, seven bits of mud from seven thresholds, seven fleeces from seven sheep, seven branches of cumin, and seven tail hairs from an old dog and tie it all to the neck with a new cord.' (*Shabbath* 67 a.)

[2] The symptoms are detailed in Matt. 17:14-21; Mark 9:14-29 and Luke 9:37-43.

[3] The parallel text of Matt. 17:15 (KJV) says: 'lunatic', and in Luke 9:38, 39, 42, spirit-possessed is used.

[4] *Oxford English Dictionary*, Second Edition, Oxford: Clarendon Press, 1989.

[5] Heb. 11:1 (NEB), (Phillips).

[6] The version of Andre Chouraqui, (*La Bible*, Desclee de Brouwer, Paris, 1985) systematically uses 'adherence' rather than 'faith' and 'to commit oneself' rather than 'to believe'.

[7] Matt. 17:15, 16. Jesus was descending from the Mountain of the Transfiguration (Matt. 17:1-15; Mark 9:2-17; Luke 9:28-38).

[8] Mark 9:19.

[9] Mark 9:23.

[10] Mark 9:24.

[11] Rom. 2:11, NEB.

[12] Rom. 12:3, NEB.

[13] Luke 18:8.

[14] 2 Cor. 4:7; Matt. 9:17.

[15] 1 Tim. 4:1, NIV.

[16] 1 Tim. 6:20, 21, NIV.

[17] 1 Tim. 6:9, 10, NIV.
[18] Matt. 4:4.
[19] Mark 9:42; Luke 17:1-4.
[20] Mark 9:28, 29 (KJV).
[21] Matt. 17:20.

At dawn

Luke 11 1-13

Dawn appears on the horizon, clearing away the shadows one by one. The world still sleeps, but birds already begin to break the early-morning silence.

The young man stands, undecided, in the bend of the path. Beyond the rock pile is a small mountain clearing. This must be the secret place. At last he has discovered where He went all those mornings while the others slept.

Why had he always feared to ask Him about it? He did not know. Something kept him from violating His privacy. However, his curiosity is great and it has finally pushed him to the point of following Him this morning. Now, standing undecided in the path, he thinks of turning back. Unable to help himself, he moves just a bit closer. Crouched behind the rock, he holds his breath for one long moment then peers over the top.

There is Jesus, praying. An overwhelming power takes hold of the disciple. He cannot look away. He seems to be kneeling not behind a rock, but upon the edge of eternity.

He has never before seen such an expression on Jesus' face. There are no lines of tension, only peace and joy. Jesus' face reflects strength, energy, power, and life. The young man trembles. This encounter so early in the morning will finally open to him Jesus' secret of peace and harmony which he has always admired and which, now more than ever, he wishes for himself.

He waits behind the rock until Jesus rises to leave. The sun has just broken from the horizon when, at last, he manages to speak. His request is simple: 'Teach me to pray.'

This disciple, like us, believed until this moment that he knew how to pray. He had been taught to pray from boyhood, and he had been praying several times each day for as long as he could remember. Prayer formed part of his everyday routine. He had prayed thousands of prayers in religious services, with the family, and in private.[1]

Prayer seemed to represent much in his life. However, the

truth is that even if he eliminated all prayer from his routine, his life would not change very much.[2] Prayer inspires his respect and awe. It gives him a comforting sense of peace. Sometimes when he has been in danger and he has appealed to God — something that he has done almost without thinking — he has always felt that at least he has done his part. And although he has never been able to prove that prayer actually works, no one has ever been able to prove the opposite.

But now, after seeing Jesus, he knows that prayer is much more.

The biblical passage recounts this story in only a few words.[3] But this small event holds one of the most surprising teachings of the gospels.

Throughout his life with Jesus, this disciple was to learn that when one is forced to abandon certain parts of religious life and keep only the essential, one thing which can be preserved in the most remote places of the earth or even in prison is prayer. One can do without everything else. But prayer is the breath of life to the soul.

His experience was to show him ever more clearly that everything else takes second place to prayer. Only prayer is essential. It is possible to be a believer without belonging to a particular religion. It is possible to believe in the dogma of a certain religion without actually practising it. *But it is not possible to have an authentic spiritual life without prayer.*

Among the believers of this world, who are becoming fewer and fewer, many practise the ceremonies of their religion. They are baptized, married, and buried by the church. And some even attend church regularly. But how many experience a deep, living, prayer life?

If religion is a relationship, then prayer is the lifeline of that relationship.

The Bible warns us of the risks we run when we neglect or withdraw from this bond with heaven. In the very first story[4] we see Satan trying to undermine Eve's confidence in her Creator, thus hoping to break off her relationship with Him. Satan tried to plant enough doubts so that Eve would act without consulting God.

After their sin, the first couple are found hiding out of shame and fear. Their relationship with God has been broken. As a direct result, their human relationship suffers. When asked why he was hiding, Adam replied: 'The woman you put here with me — she gave me some fruit from the tree . . . .'

Adam's relationship with his Creator is not what it was. It has become hostile. His relationship with Eve has also changed. She is no longer his 'suitable companion'.[5] Now she is the reason for his disgrace. He no longer sees her as being by his side but opposing him. She is no longer his partner but his opponent.

But things do not stop at human relationships. The rupture of the relationship with God also leads to the disruption of man's harmony with his environment. Adam blames Eve. And Eve blames the serpent. The equilibrium has been broken and one accuses the other, finally casting all the blame for evil upon God Himself for having created them free, or even for just creating them.

When the line of communication with God is broken, unfailingly relationships with others break down, and the weakest ends in suffering the most. Who are, after all, the final victims of human selfishness?

This brings us to the importance of prayer.

Its ultimate goal — if, indeed, it has others — is to close the gap between us and God. If communication does not take place, then prayer can become a formula, a routine, nothing more. It continues to be good because all good customs remain good, even when they are practised automatically. However, if prayer does not bring us into a relationship with anyone, then it is nothing but one more type of therapy. This kind of prayer not only fails to bring us into a privileged communion with God, but it makes us content with a gesture that does not even put us into contact with ourselves. But if prayer is an encounter, then it becomes something of utmost importance because it is the live connection with the power house of the universe. It is the source of values and of love.

Thought of like this, prayer is the recognition that we are not the centre of our world. It recognizes that the centre of our existence is there, in infinity, outside and above us. At the same time, it is so near that we can enter into contact with God at any time, in an instant. So, prayer is the recognition that to live represents something more than we can perceive in our own limited experience day to day. It means that we have access to a life-style that is unlimited. That lifestyle is only a step, only a prayer away from our small, mediocre, personal reality. That life is what makes our existence here so marvellous.

The one who does not pray is unaware of what he is missing. He has been deprived of his eternal dimension. His life may be morally correct and full of values, yet it will lack depth because he has excluded from it the very thing which could raise him to a higher level of relationships.

Praying means opening oneself to divine power.[6]

C. S. Lewis authored a humorous book[7] which illustrates this point.

The action is set in hell where a new demon has been given his first mission on earth. It consists of tempting a young, naturally good, and exceptionally healthy young man until he succeeds in destroying him.

The young man has had a born-again experience. This infuriates the devil who makes the young man his special mark. The case is so difficult that the young demon must consult his uncle, a demon with experience. The book is composed of the supposed correspondence between these two demons.

The more cunning demon recommends to his nephew that he concentrate his attack upon the young man's prayer life. The idea is to block prayer by whatever means.

Firstly, the demon must make sure that the young man does not pray. He must keep him so busy doing good things that he does not have time to pray. And if he should pray, then the demon must make sure that the prayer is as brief and as routine as possible. The idea is to keep the young man from communicating with 'the Enemy', because once he has entered into contact with God all demons are rendered powerless.

Secondly, if the demon cannot keep the young man from praying, he must, at all costs, make sure that the young man loses his desire to pray. He must make him too tired or too discouraged so that he puts the prayer off for another time.

Finally, if after all this the young man insists on praying, he must be distracted so that he cannot concentrate.

Lack of time, lack of desire, and lack of concentration. Aren't these our problems as well?

Imagine a friend who never wishes to talk with you and who doesn't pay attention when you talk to him! Would you put up with him for very long? However, this kind of behaviour, which we loathe so much in others, is all too often a part of our relationship with God.

When my children were young and learning to pray, more than once they knelt at their bed and prayed: 'Thank you for this food we eat.'

Or we would be seated round the table for breakfast and they would pray: 'Keep us safe throughout this night.'

While we smile at such childish behaviour, it does point out our misunderstanding of prayer. The child is reciting a formula. He is acting out a conditioned response, putting the prayer cassette on 'play'. He does not have a clear idea of entering into contact with anyone.

The same thing happens to us. We forget that prayer is more than something we recite. We do not understand that it is something we live; that it is more communion than communication.

If we were aware of this fact, prayer would cease to be routine, pressured, forced. If we would only stop to realize that in this privileged moment of prayer the Creator of the Universe is willing to listen to us, to talk with us, to grant us His undivided attention for as long as we desire, our spiritual lives would be transformed.

One of my most humiliating and yet enriching experiences with the gospels has been the realization that some of my prayers, and some that I often hear from others, are actually pagan prayers.[8]

The ancient pagans offered sacrifices and chants to their gods in order to ask for something, to appease them for something, or to change the gods' attitudes.[9] Do not our prayers, at times, seem like great efforts designed to sensitize God to things which do not appear to interest Him?

Many of our prayers seem especially pagan because we use the imperative form: orders and demands. We ask; we beg; we supplicate in an effort to make Him act. We often pray as if, were it not for God, were it not for this Great Obstacle, things in life would go much better. We pray as if God were a distant tyrant with whom we have to plead in order to lift Him out of lethargy and indifference.[10]

'We ask you to bring peace to the world.'

How dare we accuse Him of indifference to world peace when He has been trying to convince us of the stupidity of violence for thousands of years!

If we were to record some of our prayers and analyse them, we would realize that we often believe ourselves to be better than God.

'Dear Lord, have pity upon the orphans . . . the poor . . . and the needy.'

In fact, we are asking Him to be more 'human'. We are asking Him to react because, compared with ourselves, He seems to lack sensitivity. He seems not to care enough. And then, when a flash of His divine love and of His divine suffering over the misery of the world finally reaches us and moves us, we run to Him with the news and pray: 'Do something for these ones in need!'

Unconsciously, we are asking that God intervene in our place. It is so much easier to pray, 'Be with the poor', than to help them ourselves. We believe that if we pray, 'Remember those in need', that frees us from all obligation. We believe that our prayer is of great value. After all, poverty is rooted in something outside ourselves, isn't it? Wouldn't it be more honest to say, 'Lord, when I think of the poor around me, I must ask you to help me discover what I can do for them. How can I help to remedy this injustice which you hate and for which my lack of love is to blame?'

It is so sad that prayer has turned out to be our way

of reminding God of His duties: 'Lord, remember your church.'

Who is in danger of forgetting the church, is *He* or are *we*?

Fortunately, God, in His mercy, listens and understands in spite of what we say. But if we wish to deepen our relationship with Him, we cannot be content to chant our prayers routinely. We must ask Him to continue to have patience with us and to teach us to pray. Paul said, 'We do not know what we ought to pray, but the Spirit himself intercedes for us with groans that words cannot express.'[11] The more we understand our need to relearn how to pray, the more sensitive we will be to the voice of the Holy Spirit. When we pray in a superficial way, He will help us change the tone and will help us concentrate. So our prayer will begin to sound like a real conversation with an intelligent being. We will begin to understand our need for God and for others and will begin to see ourselves for what we really are.

Praying is not so much talking as listening. It is not so much asking as receiving. It isn't calling God as much as it is responding to His call.

What a shame that we often limit ourselves to praying our prayer without waiting for His answer!

The story goes that a little boy on a doorstep was stretching on tiptoe to reach the doorbell. A kindly man lifted him up. The boy rang the bell and immediately wriggled free. 'Now we run!' he shouted back as he ran off.

I'm afraid that sometimes our prayers must sound something like that. We ring the bell, but when He opens the door, we've already gone on to other things.

Prayer isn't trying to manipulate God, nor is it designed to make Him change His mind and do our will. Prayer is our endeavour to understand His will and to offer ourselves in His service.

The prayer which impressed me the most was that of an old gentleman, and it went like this: 'Lord, it's John here.'

A precious prayer.

'Here I am. I know there are others more qualified to carry

out your will. I know there are others more able, more reliable. Perhaps I'm not much good to you. But here I am. Teach me what I can do.'

This, finally, begins to sound like prayer.

Does God always answer our prayers? Some teach that this depends upon our faith, our sincerity, our humility and our availability. I would say that God always answers us. However, as our Father, He is too good and too intelligent to give us all we ask, even when we express it with total sincerity and even when we insist. Sometimes He gives us only what is best for us. And sometimes His answer is 'No'.

Once a student confided to me, 'I've prayed many times but very rarely have I received an answer.'

I don't know whether or not all my student's prayers were answered. What I do know is that if there are requests that go unanswered, they are far outnumbered by those which God has made to us. Before His apparent silence, the only intelligent response is to maintain the relationship, knowing that He will help us to accept the reality in which we live and will help us move beyond it.

To pray without ceasing[12] does not mean that God will give in only after a long and repetitive insistence on our part. Rather, it means that we can feel His presence at any time and in any circumstance: washing dishes, driving a car, working behind a machine, or studying in a classroom. Praying without ceasing means that it is not absolutely necessary to close the eyes or kneel down. What matters is our inner disposition, not the position of our eyelids or our knees. Praying without ceasing is, quite simply, keeping ourselves open to dialogue, open to listen to Him, open to serve Him.

And so if prayer means coming close to God and opening ourselves to His influence, the most enriching times will normally be our private encounters, our private moments, those privileged times reserved only for Him.

Some wonder, with a certain amount of irony, why prayer is necessary if God knows everything anyway. Prayer is sharing rather than informing. We bring our needs to the Fountain of solutions. We connect our lives to the Source of life. We widen our understanding in the Fountain of

Wisdom. We purify our human love, always so conditional and selfish, in the crucible of generous and unconditional love.

A relationship does not consist of talking to God without sharing our lives with Him. This is even true in the prayer of confession. God doesn't ask us to report to Him our shortcomings because He needs to know about them — but because we need to share them with Him. Confession is necessary for our spiritual growth; not only for the pardon and peace that it brings us, but because it forces us to take time in self-evaluation. By opening ourselves sincerely before God, by meditating upon His will, we see ourselves more clearly. It is then that God can influence our lives and help us to rise above our problems. Prayer is more than simple meditation.

Cosmonauts know that during their space walking it is imperative that they maintain their link with base. In order to undertake the smallest duty they need constant communication. To lose this communication means almost immediate destruction. However, since the consequences of separation from God are not seen immediately in our lives, we give little importance to the maintenance of the lifeline with our Centre of Energy.

Our spiritual perception is so shortsighted and breaks down so easily. Like the disciple in our story, many of us need to find the Master and say:

'Teach me to pray. Help me to live in relationship with you. Teach me to see how much I need this constant encounter, this life-giving meditation, this transmission of energy in order to recharge my batteries of strength, values, happiness, and love, so that my life will be connected with yours and will be more abundant.'

---

¹The prescribed custom — apart from the ritual prayers which formed part of the daily religious services, or of the Sabbath ceremonies, as well as those of the other festivals and special occasions — called for a minimum of three times for daily prayer (morning, noon, and night), along with the prayers (called *berakoth*, or 'blessings') before eating or drinking (*Birkhot ha Nehenin*) and the prayers prayed before fulfilling any commandment (*Birkhot ha Mitzvot*). (*Berakhot* 1:1-9:5.)

68   AT DAWN

²Although Israel had, without doubt, a repertoire of beautiful and profound prayers from ancient times (the book of Psalms, along with the prayers of the Synagogue), these tended to be recited in Hebrew, a language nearly dead at that time since the only ones speaking it were scholars. However, it was preserved as the liturgic language in the same way that Latin was used by the Catholic tradition for hundreds of years. Even today, if a *berakah* is to have validity in another language, it must contain the original idea found in the Hebrew text as well as contain the basic formula 'Blessed be . . . God and King of the Universe . . . .' (R. Siegel and M. S. Strassfeld, *The First Jewish Catalog*, Philadelphia: The Jewish Publication Society of America, 1980, page 150.

³The gospels record many occasions in which Jesus retires to the mountain alone in order to pray: Matt. 14:23; Mark 6:46; Luke 6:12. Our text is based on Luke 11:1.

⁴Gen. 3:1-24.

⁵Gen. 2:18-23 (GNB).

⁶Paul says that 'we, who with unveiled faces all reflect the Lord's glory, are being transformed into his likeness with ever-increasing glory, which comes from the Lord, who is the Spirit.' (2 Cor. 3:18, NIV.)

⁷C. S. Lewis, *The Screwtape Letters*, 1976, pages 33-35.

⁸Jesus Christ warns us about two types of pseudo-prayers: the formal chants (Matt. 6:5, 6) and the pagan prayers (Matt. 6:7, 8). The type of prayer recommended by Jesus is a model of authenticity, of power, and of reality (Matt. 6:9-15).

⁹As an example of pagan prayer, let us look at a prayer of Emperor Augustus: 'According to the regulations written in the Sibiline books . . . we offer a sacrifice of nine sheep and nine goats. We ask that you be favourable, in war and in peace, to the Roman Empire, to the School of the Fifteen, to me, to my house, and to my family. Accept with favour this sacrifice . . . given as ritual demands.' (A. M. di Nola, *Le Livre d'or de la priere de tous les peuples et des tous les temps*, Paris: Seghers, M. V. 37, 1982, pages 220, 221.

¹⁰In my reflections on this point I owe much to Louis Everly, *La priere d'un homme moderne*, (Paris 1969), pages 13-20.

¹¹Rom. 8:26, 27, NIV.

¹²Regarding the reasons for 'prayer without ceasing', that is never to cease communicating with God, see Luke 11:5-7; 18:1; 21:36; Rom. 12:12; Eph. 6:18; and 1 Thess. 5:17.

On a trip

Their luggage, a hodgepodge of bags and bundles, lies strewn along the side of the road. Excited goodbyes rise above the noisy hubbub as the young travellers ready themselves for the journey. Boisterous chatter belies their underlying anxiety, their fear of the unknown and the unfamiliar.

Jesus pauses a moment in His playing with the children and looks about to see how the preparations are proceeding. He does not appear rushed and nervous, though He understands the excitement of His fellow travellers. He is used to life on the road; and yet this new route leads Him to an uncertain destination upon the horizon. He smiles encouragingly at His companions, and then returns to the children who are playfully holding on to His legs as if to keep Him from leaving. He lingers with them a few minutes longer, laughing and joking and hugging them.[1]

Jesus has chosen an itinerant ministry based on the needs and desires of others. His vocation is to search for man, to wait for him, and to invite him to travel the road to happiness with Him.

It is time to leave. All the goodbyes have been said, and an expectant hush settles on the gathering. With one last farewell wave, Jesus starts off, motioning His friends to follow Him. The young men pick up their bundles and head off down the road. No one asks about the final destination. From their short experience with Jesus, they know that each new trip holds adventure and uncertainty.

Not long into their journey a stranger comes running to catch up with them[2] and bows respectfully before Jesus. He is obviously anxious to consult Jesus about something. The urgency in his look makes the Master stop. A counsellor by profession, Jesus withdraws to the side of the road where He can give this stranger His undivided attention.

The young man in his fine clothes[3] seems out of place on the dusty road. He does not belong here. But he is young and impulsive.[4] Hearing that Jesus is in town, he must run out to meet Him on foot. There is no time to saddle up the horses. Now he breaks in upon the group of strangers without a thought of his position or status.[5]

He is looking for a spiritual guide. Without doubt, he has had many famous and eminent teachers, yet compared with them, Jesus seems genuinely better. He is more balanced, more sincere, and certainly happier. Jesus has what the young man desires: moral strength and peace of mind and soul.

Out of breath, he bows before Jesus and addressed Him as 'Good Teacher.'

Jesus asks for an explanation: 'Why do you call me good? No one is good except God alone.'[6]

According to some interpretations, in this way Jesus is declaring His divinity.[7] It's as if He had said: 'If you call me good and God is the only good Being, that means you understand, or must understand, that I am God.'

But this explanation is not convincing because it is not in character with the practice of Jesus elsewhere in the gospels.

Instead, it appears that He is saying: 'Listen, if anyone is good, as you seem to think I am, it is only as a result of his contact with the Fountain of Goodness. Your problem can be solved only by God. If I intervene, it is only because I think I can help you to understand better who God is, what He can do for you, and what He expects from you.'

The young man is not put off. He has come to ask a question and he asks it: 'What must I do to inherit eternal life?'

He has been educated well. He does not ask, 'What must I do to *earn* eternal life?' From a correct theological position, he chooses the word 'inherit' which means to receive freely something for which one has never worked, or to accept something that is given to one. He knows that salvation is something which cannot be earned but may only be received.

This intelligent young man, heir to a great fortune, is obviously dissatisfied. He possesses many things, but he cannot seem to achieve happiness and peace of mind. His wealth gives him security in this life, but what of the life to come?

Filled with unease and dogged by anxiety, he comes to Jesus for an answer. We know nothing of earlier meetings. We do not know if he has followed Jesus from afar or more closely during a long or short period of time. We know only that he is filled with pressing problems, with dread and anguish. He has spent much time searching his heart and even more in smothering the pride which has kept him from presenting his fears to Jesus. Now, when he *finally* decides to come to the Master, he very nearly misses the opportunity! His question does not stem from mere intellectual doubts. It reveals an intense inner struggle and a painful undercurrent of doubts and fears.

We recognize ourselves in this young man. Too often our hands are filled with material things while our hearts are spiritually poor. We, too, come to Jesus in search of an abundant life.

The young man's question hangs in the air, waiting to be answered. Jesus realizes where his real problem lies, and He begins by reiterating the central themes of the Scriptures. He chooses from the commandments some which refer to human relationships.

'God gives us the best philosophy of life so that we will be happy. You know the Scriptures. Undoubtedly, you know the commandments by heart: do not commit adultery; do not murder; do not steal; do not give false testimony; honour your father and mother. The best thing is to allow God to lead you in all that you do.'[8]

The young man considers himself to be a practising believer, and he is disappointed with Jesus' answer. There seems to be nothing new in this teaching. This cannot be the formula for peace and serenity. In a very different tone of voice he answers: 'All these I have kept since I was a boy. I already know that the world would be a better place if everyone obeyed the commandments. What I need you to tell me is why I feel so empty inside, even though I try to practise my beliefs. I take my religious life seriously. I obey the law the best I can. I go to church. I try to pray regularly, and yet I am dissatisfied. I feel the need for something more. I cannot find fulfilment in what I do. What do I lack? What is missing?'

Jesus sees much promise in the young man, and He cannot help but feel love for him.[9] Measuring His words carefully, Jesus says, as He would to one for whom He is wishing the best: 'You still lack one thing . . . .'[10]

The young man's heart misses a beat as he waits for the long-awaited answer. His mind searches frantically for that one thing. Certainly he did not expect the sentence to end with what seems to be the hardest instruction in all the gospel.

'"Go, and sell everything you have and give to the poor, and you will have treasure in heaven. Then come, follow me."'

Surprising paradox. In order to fill his emptiness, he must rid himself of all his plenty. Hard words, but logical ones. If what you have does not make you happy, then leave it for something better.

Jesus knows that happiness cannot be found in selfishness. If we continue to be the axis around which our world turns, then we can never be completely satisfied. We will always lack the essentials. Love of self never leads anywhere. The 'I' can never be satisfied. Only God can satisfy the thirst of the human heart. If we really want to be sure of eternity we must allow Him into our lives.

Jesus continues: 'You know the commandments. But do you know the greatest one? The greatest one is "Love the Lord your God with all your heart and with all your soul and with all your mind." And the second is just as important, "Love your neighbour as yourself." '[11]

The true spiritual life is measured by these rules. Religion that limits itself to mere doctrines has shown throughout history that it has become lifeless and stunted. Faith which feeds on love can never become 'the opium of the people' or an instrument used to manipulate the minds of others.

We notice that Jesus does not talk of religion in terms of 'to believe', but rather 'to love'. For Him, a believer is not one who is faithful to a set of beliefs but rather one who is faithful to God and to his fellowman. Of course, faithfulness to God supposes the acceptance of His teachings. But, ultimately, what makes one a follower of Jesus is not one's declaration of faith but one's life of service. What distinguishes a Christian from others is his relationship with them.

'"All men will know that you are my disciples if you love one another."'[12]

The Christian is one who tries to live and love as Christ does. Unlike the many sects who define their religion in terms of orthodoxy, Christ, the Founder of Christianity, is more concerned with relationships and attitudes.

Jesus is really telling this wealthy young man: 'You lack only one thing. Share what you have and follow Me. You do not need to learn new religious exercises. What you need to do is to exercise your humanity. You do not need to follow new rules. You need to take a new direction in your life.'[13]

Those who haven't experienced a personal faith think that a believer is one who stagnates or submits to traditions. Jesus teaches that faith means a beginning, a new start. For Jesus, a Christian is one who accepts God's invitation and is capable of leaving everything behind in order to follow Him, wherever He leads — even if it means going beyond the well-worn tracks of popular beliefs.

Jesus' invitation to this young man was similar to God's call to Abraham. Abraham was called 'the father of the believers' because he had the courage to answer the divine call. Leaving his heathen surroundings he set off towards the Promised Land. Neither the beginning nor the trip itself was important, only the destination. By accepting the risks involved in attempting such a trip, he discovered a new road and a new horizon. He began a new life, paradoxically more secure because it was guided by God, and certainly freer without the dead weight of his past. It was more authentic, being based on truth, and fuller by being open to the direction of the Life-giver.

Like many, this young man has travelled through life without a clear direction. He has allowed himself to be carried along by the crowd. That is, until he finds the Guide for whom he has been searching. Now Jesus waits for him to react positively to His offer, but there is no sign of acceptance.

The young man, after hearing Jesus' words, bows his head in sorrow because he is a man of great wealth.[14] He does not understand that Jesus is not driving him to ruin, but that He is offering the best of all worlds. He does not understand that he would be exchanging his wealth for riches that would continue to increase as he continued to give. He does not understand that the poorest of all people are those who have only wealth. He does not understand that happiness comes from giving, not from receiving.[15] He does not know that to follow Christ on His trip is worth more than living in a palace without Him.

His indecision proves that although he is powerful, he is not free. He belongs to his belongings. All of his potential is chained to a current account and some property titles. The wealth of today prohibits him from inheriting eternity.

He shows by his actions that he is not as young as he appears to be. His wealth has made him so old in thought that he is incapable of beginning with Jesus the trip of a lifetime. Nor is he as rich as he believes himself to be, because what he has is not enough to give him happiness. All the wealth of the world cannot give him the one thing which can keep him young and wealthy for ever.

As the disciples begin to move on again, Jesus stands looking sadly back at the retreating young man who heads in the wrong direction. He is left behind and is lost, perhaps in all senses, on the horizon of his sedentary immobility, unable to break his chains of gold.

We have begun the journey, and it has brought us here to a standstill. Like the young man we, too, need to review our spiritual roots. We need to uproot the selfishness which is so deeply embedded in our souls and which makes us live only for ourselves in the midst of so many needy.

Jesus returns to the road. He turns to us and asks: 'Will you follow Me wherever I lead or will you, too, leave Me?'[16]

'The synoptic gospels (the first three) place this encounter with the rich young ruler immediately after the episode where Jesus interrupts His preaching to talk with the children. (Matt. 19:13-15, 16-22; Mark 10:13-16, 17-22; Luke 18:15-17, 18-23.)

²Mark 10:17.

³Luke 18:18 defines him as 'a ruler', that is, someone who held a prominent position in the government or a brilliant lawyer. (See Mark 10:17-22; John 3:1.)

⁴According to an ancient rabbinical rule of etiquette, 'A respectable man must never walk with his head held high because he must not appear arrogant; he must not swagger lest he appear effeminate, he must *not run in public* so as not to appear silly, and he must not scowl, thus appearing annoyed. He must look downwards as if he were praying and walk with purpose as if on his way to an important event.' (Maimonides, *Yad De'ot* 5:8.)

Perhaps the reason for the details of the story is to show us that the young man involved acted with a certain amount of immaturity. (Matt. 19:20 says that he was a young man.)

⁵Luke 18:23; Mark 10:22; Matt. 19:22.

⁶There is no record of any rabbi who was referred to in this way. (W. Lane, *The Gospel of Mark*, Eerdmans: Grand Rapids, 1982, page 365.) In the rabbinical literature this expression appears only once and was pronounced by a heavenly voice in a dream (b *Ta'anith* 24 b).

⁷This interpretation was known at the end of the second century by Irenaeus of Lyons (*Adversus Haereses* 1:20, 2).

⁸In the biblical meaning, the commandments are the expression of divine love (Ps. 111: 119), because they look out for our well-being. By observing them, the believer lives in harmony with God and with mankind (2 John 4-6). Since God is love (1 John 4:16), His commandments summarize love (Matt. 22:36-40; Rom. 13:8-10.)

⁹Mark 10:21.

¹⁰Jesus always makes the spiritual journey acceptable to those who search for truth. To this young man He says, 'You only lack one thing', and He surprises a scribe when He says: '"You are not far from the kingdom of God."' (Mark 12:34, NIV.)

¹¹Matt. 22:34-40. Jesus considers these relationships so linked together that He refuses to answer a question as limited as, Which is the first commandment? without mentioning the second as well. In order to summarize the law (understood in the biblical sense, that is, as the whole of divine teachings), Jesus didn't refer to the Decalogue (Exod. 20:1-17; Deut. 5:6-21) the text most usually referred to, but rather to two passages considered as basic by the rabbis (specifically Deut. 6:5 and Lev. 19:18) which summarize between them the two great sections of the Decalogue.

According to Israelite tradition, '613 commandments were given to Moses at Sinai: 365 prohibitions, one for each day of the solar year, and 248 commands, one for each part of the human body.' (*Makkoth* 23 b).

Which of these commandments should be considered the 'first' or the 'principal' one was often discussed in Jesus' day. According to some, the first commandment was 'to believe in God' (*Encyclopaedia Judaica*, Keter,

Jerusalem, 1972, t. 5, cols. 760-783). However, in practice the law of circumcision occupied this place since it was the first commandment given to Israel in the person of Abraham (Gen. 17:11, 12; 21:4), and the first through which all men must pass in order to become part of the people of God. Circumcision was considered so important that 'without the blood of this covenant neither heaven nor earth would exist, since Abraham was circumcised on the tenth day of the month Tishri, which later became the Day of Atonement when all the sins of Israel were pardoned.' (*Pirkei*, R. Eliezer, 29.) According to some experts, the observance of this law, above all others, has been what has insured the survival of the Israelites over the centuries (cf. Spinoza, *Tractatus Theologico-politicus* 3:53; *Encyclopaedia Judaica*, t. 5, col. 572). It isn't strange that the first Jewish Christians defended this belief so vigorously (Acts 15:1; Gal. 5:1-15).

The prevalent belief at that time, however, was that all the commandments were of equal importance, even if some appeared to be of lesser significance: 'Let the most insignificant commandment be as important to you as the most significant one.' (See Deut. 12:28; 13:18.)

If there is one commandment which appears to be emphasized in the Bible, it is the Sabbath. It is the first commandment to be observed after the Creation of the world by God Himself (Gen. 2:1-3; Exod. 20:8-11; Deut. 5:12-15); it is the only commandment designed as a perpetual covenant and eternal sign of identity for the people of God (Exod. 31:13-17); the prophets emphasize it over the rest (Neh. 9:13, 14); and even refer to it as a symbol and a guarantee of salvation (Isa. 56:1-7). The value of the Sabbath is such that someone once said that 'when Israel would observe the Sabbath as dictated only once, the Messiah would come.' (*Exodus Rabbah* 25:12.)

The uniqueness of Jesus' teaching is not found in the idea that love for God and love for fellow man are needed in order to fulfil the law. This was already recognized by both the Old Testament and Judaism of His day. The revolutionary idea which Jesus put forth was that Love was the summation of the Divine Law. 'Love is the fulfilling of the Law.' (Rom. 13:10.)

[12] John 13:35.

[13] To cut the cords that bind us doesn't mean conquering our faults. Not only do we *not* need to conquer our faults in order to come to Christ, but we are totally unable to do so. To try would be to fall into the most devilish trap (according to biblical language) that there can be. The only thing we need to conquer is our hesitancy in giving ourselves to Him. Victory over our problems will come later because Jesus will be our guide and the power in our lives. In John 1:12 it says that 'to all who were willing, He gave power to become sons of God.'

[14] Luke 18:23.

[15] Acts 20:35.

[16] The word 'religion' comes from the Latin *religare* which means 'to unite again'. Its primary theological meaning is that of establishing a relationship with God or of renewing a broken relationship.

At home

The house of Lazarus and his sisters, Martha and Mary, is a haven of peace for Jesus; a refuge from the heat of the desert and the demands of the bustling city. Wishing to rest among friends before His last difficult assignment in Jerusalem, Jesus pauses at Bethany.[1]

On His arrival Mary and Martha both hurry to welcome Him. Mary offers Jesus water to refresh Himself.[2] Then, with childlike amity she leads Him to the patio.

Jesus gratefully sits back among the plants and the cushions. From this comfortable spot He looks out on the neatly-tiered vineyards. Olive and fig trees dot the hills[3] which block Jerusalem from view.[4] Jesus knows that death awaits Him beyond those hills and He gazes at them with a certain sadness. Mary senses that Jesus needs friendship and she sits down among the pots of mint, dill, and cumin,[5] offering herself as a disciple in silent sympathy.[6]

Unlike other teachers of His day, Jesus accepts women into His group of disciples; and some very prominent women are counted among His friends. Although Mary does not seem to have anything in common with the others, He accepts her. He knows how much she has changed.

To others she continues to be the pampered girl who has ruined her life; the crazy, demon-possessed girl who never knew how to choose what was right; the unsettled girl, marked forever by her past indiscretions.[7] Even her recent devotion to Jesus appears to be one more whim . . . a phase of a different sort that will, like all the others, pass with time.

But Jesus knows that this time she has begun a journey from which no one can discourage her.

Always different from her sister, Martha cannot hide her nervousness at Jesus' unexpected arrival. She, too, wants to provide the best possible hospitality; and she would have preferred it if He had stayed in the sitting-room, the fitting place for an honoured guest. The near presence of even her best friends makes her nervous.[8] A typical housekeeper, she likes things to be done her way.

She rushes to light the fire, to get water, to pick a basket of fresh fruit, to pull out the best tablecloth from the large chest. She runs from the garden to the woodpile and from the living-room to the well. In the meantime, the fire is crackling and the water is boiling in the pot.

Red-faced and perspiring, Martha glances angrily at Mary who, unaware of it all, sits listening to Jesus.[9] Women were not expected to be interested in religion. Martha, therefore, regarded Mary's devotion as excessive and bothersome.

Martha tries to attract Mary's attention. She purposefully clangs the pots. She signals to her from the kitchen. When she passes by, she first brushes up against Mary and then jostles her.

When Mary does not respond, Martha explodes. She justifies her actions by contrasting her industry with the inactivity of her sister. Filled with resentment, she even forgets her good manners and loudly berates her Guest. 'Lord, how can you be so insensitive when I am trying so hard to please you? Don't you care that my sister has left me to do the work by myself? Tell her to help me!'[10]

Martha has lost all sense of proportion. She sees her sister Mary as the typical new convert who is obsessed with the spiritual insights of the teacher, and she prides herself on her practical efficiency.

The truth is that Martha does not understand Jesus who, she thinks, wastes His time on unimportant issues. Although she would have liked to, she has never really been able to confide in Him. Without realizing it, Martha is working as an alternative to facing up to her frustrations. She is goaded by the sight of Mary's paying close attention to their honoured Guest.

Martha has misjudged her sister. In her way, Mary is also serving Jesus. Today she has not helped in preparing the meal but she is planning to spend a year's salary on a pound of spikenard to anoint His feet.[11] Mary is the one who will accompany Him to the cross.[12] She will show more courage than His disciples who will have vowed not to forsake Him. She will be the first to whom the risen Lord will appear.[13]

Mary understands that she has much to learn, and she anxiously desires the Master to teach her. She knows that He can transform her life. She has learned through experience that Jesus has come to serve and not to be served.

Jesus does not answer Martha's rebuke as most men of His time would have done. He knows both sisters well; and although it appears that He is taking sides, He does not defend either of them; neither does He defend Himself. Jesus comes immediately to the point. 'Martha, Martha, you are worried and upset about many things, but only one thing is needed. Mary has chosen what is better, and it will not be taken away from her.'

If Martha nervously busies herself with the preparations and aggressively lashes out at others, it is because something is lacking in her perception of reality. She puts things — a well-laid table, a tasty dinner — before eternal values. She places emphasis on the things of little consequence before her relationship with her Saviour.

Although she cooks for Him, she fails to supply his needs. She does not understand what He wants of her. Her interest really does not focus on her Guest but on herself: on her dinner, her image, her prestige.

Jesus does not reprove Martha for her activity nor does He scorn her interest in domestic duties. He will enjoy cooking for His friends on the shores of Galilee after His resurrection.[14] He simply invites her to rethink her values. Jesus does not reproach Martha for what she does but for what she leaves undone. He does not question her diligence but her priorities. He shows her that her activities, although good, deprive her of something better. She gives too much importance to the secondary because she does not know how, or does not have the courage, to face the essential. She prefers a formal relationship at a formal dinner to a face-to-face encounter with the One who is the Way, the Truth and the Life.

The more Martha works, the more she suffers. Her irritability creates a wall which blocks her relationship with Jesus. Instead of coming closer to Him, she tries to avoid Him. Since she does not really know Jesus, she believes that the most important thing is to supply his material needs. She does not yet understand that what matters is what He can do for her.

Mary and Martha represent two different attitudes. Mary wants to be with Jesus. His presence gives her peace and serenity. She listens, learns and is happy. Martha, absorbed in her work, loses out. Nervous and worried, she grumbles and criticizes. Her own agitation places her in opposition to her sister and pulls her further away from Jesus.

We, too, have our priorities all mixed up. We lose ourselves in our busy, technological world. We work to conquer outer space but not to control our inner beings. We strive to control natural forces but not our own willpower. We limit atomic energy, but not our sexual drive. We masterfully conquer the force of gravity but ignore the power of habit. We drive the most sophisticated cars but cannot guide ourselves. We beat untold epidemics, but stubbornly choose not to rise above our prejudices. We make incredible connections in complicated electronic circuits, but we do not know how to establish normal relationships with members of our own families.

Perhaps, like Martha, what we most need is to call a halt to all our activity. Perhaps we need to search for peace in Jesus. Perhaps, like Mary, when we find ourselves alone with Him, we will understand that the only essential thing is our relationship to Him.[15]

---

[1] Text based on Luke 10:38-42. Bethany in those days was a small town located less than one and a half miles to the south-east of Jerusalem (John 11:18 says fifteen furlongs, or 15 x 606 feet) along the road to Jericho. The gospels mention that Jesus visited the house of Lazarus, Martha and Mary in Bethany on numerous occasions, either coming from the Judean desert or returning from Jerusalem (Matt. 21:17; Mark 11:1; 12; Luke 19:29, etc.)

[2] One of the duties of the wife or daughter was to wash the face, hands, and feet of the head of the house (*Tos. Kiddushin* 1:11; b. *Kethuboth* 61a).

82   AT HOME

³This description is based upon the landscape which is still visible today from what is called 'the house of Lazarus'.

⁴From Bethany, Jerusalem was hidden from view by the famous Mount of Olives.

⁵It was normal to grow herbs and spices such as mint, dill and cumin at home (Matt. 23:23).

⁶The act of a woman adopting the attitude of a disciple (considered only a masculine trait) was unheard of until Jesus accepted it. Even so, the gospels speak little of His female disciples. However, Luke does say that they were numerous and that some were of high social class such as Joanna, the wife of Herod's steward (Luke 8:1-3).

⁷Many biblical scholars identify Mary of Bethany with the woman caught in adultery (Luke 7:36-50) and with Mary Magdalene who had seven demons cast out of her (Luke 8:2). In *Testament of Reuben* 2:1, it says that in cases of multiple possession, 'that of the seven impure spirits, the first is sexual promiscuity'.

⁸Rules of etiquette prohibited a man's meeting alone or talking privately with a woman (*Kiddushin* 4:12 b; 81a) or even talking to her at all, except in the most minimal way. Jose ben Johanan of Jerusalem, one of the most ancient respected scribes (around the year 150 BC) ordered: 'Don't talk much with a woman . . . not even with your wife.' (*Aboth* 1:5.) From that we can understand the disciples' disbelief upon seeing Jesus in conversation with the Samaritan woman (John 4:27). Philo, a contemporary of Jesus, said: 'Women must stay at home and live a hidden life. Young girls must stay within the inner rooms of the house with the door which accesses the rooms of the men as their limit. Married women should not step beyond the patio door . . . in order to avoid the looks from men, even from close relatives.' (*De specialibus legibus* 3:169.) In actual practice those 'ideals' do not seem to have been carried to those extremes in real life.

⁹In that society women tended to maintain themselves aloof from the majority of religious rites, since it was believed that they were bound only by the prohibitions of the Torah with the exception of the three of Lev. 19:27 and 21:1-2 (*Kiddushin* 1:7). They were excused from almost all of the positive precepts, that is, from all those which were established to determine proper use of time (*Kiddushin* 1:7) such as the obligation to go to Jerusalem in pilgrimage during the feasts, to attend religious services (*Hagigah* 1:1), the recitation of certain prayers (*Berakoth* 3:3), and, above all, to study the Torah.

¹⁰Courtesy demanded that one 'remain quiet before someone of greater wisdom, not interrupt the conversation, not put pressure on the other for an answer, and only ask appropriate and important questions' (*Aboth* 5:7).

Respect for parents applied equally to teachers. When a son or a disciple felt compelled to question the behaviour of the adult, he must do so in private. The method recommended is as follows: 'Father, the Torah says in such and such verse . . . ', leaving the teacher or parent to draw his own conclusions. (*Kiddushin* 32 a.)

[11] John 12:1-8 says that Mary anointed Jesus with 'a pound of spikenard perfume which Judas valued at a price of 300 denari'. We can guess at the value of this gift when we understand that a denari was the equivalent of an average salary for a day's work. (c.f. Matt. 26:6-13; Mark 14:3-9.)

[12] Matt. 27:55, 56; Mark 15:40, 41; Luke 23:49.

[13] Matt. 28:1-10; Mark 16:1-8; Luke 24:1-11; John 20:11-18.

[14] John 21:4-9.

[15] The key is to be able to say as Paul did: 'For me to live is Christ.' (Phil. 1:21.)

Along the way

The young men slouch dejectedly alongside the road. Tired from the journey and upset by what has happened in the last town, they have no more strength to go on. Other days they would have continued until dusk. But this afternoon they prefer to rest. But where? Certainly they cannot camp in the open. The thieving gangs of the region would be sure to find them.

Things had gone badly in the last town. They had been identified as Jews and had been forced to leave.[1] It was difficult to pass through Samaria unnoticed. Fires of ancestral hatred, passed on from fathers to sons and continually fanned by quarrels and disputes, burned into the Samaritans' minds a special sense when it came to recognizing Jews.

The disciples would never have risked asking for lodging in the last town. It was Jesus who had persuaded them, moved by His all-embracing spirit. They could not understand Him. They admired His courage, His sense of justice, just about everything. But they did not understand His incredible patience towards His enemies.[2]

They have left all to follow Him, but it is difficult for them to follow Him in everything. Two things are particularly problematic for them. They find it difficult to forget what others will say and they cannot seem to stop hating their enemies.[3]

When the Samaritans closed the doors of their town, the disdain opened afresh the old wounds of hatred in the disciples' hearts. They were not angry because they had been thrown out of the town. No, they had already expected as much from Samaritans. But the fact that the townsmen had rejected Jesus, who had come to help them, made the disciples' blood boil. Revenge seemed the only appropriate response. '"Lord, may we call down fires from heaven to burn them up?"'[4]

Their beliefs do not allow them to understand the fact that God rarely needs to punish anybody. They do not understand that the townspeople, by rejecting Jesus, are punishing themselves and condemning themselves.[5] Jesus is on His final journey to Jerusalem and the cross. He will never pass this way again.

'You do not know what kind of spirit you are of, for the Son of Man did not come to destroy men's lives, but to save them.'[6]

The unexpected reproach from Jesus has left them ashamed and embarrassed. Painfully, silently, the disciples resume their journey. With heads down, they start out towards another town. Certainly following Jesus is not always what they had imagined it to be.[7]

Jesus continues a short distance ahead thinking sad, lonely thoughts. Those who do not know Him do not want to receive Him, and those who follow Him are more willing to destroy than to save. Is there hope for any of them? He, too, feels discouraged. Yet He stops and waits in order to continue the journey with them.

Three unexpected encounters change the tense mood. Jesus meets three men who desire to follow Him. However, He will answer their seemingly rational and understandable conditions with irrational and disconcerting directness.[8]

The first to draw near is a scribe.[9] He is so impressed by the Nazarene that he offers, apparently wholeheartedly, to follow Jesus: 'Teacher, I will follow you wherever you go!'

But Jesus realizes that this impetuous young man is about to embark upon something totally unknown. Without rejecting the young man's apparent willingness, Jesus forces him to reflect upon what awaits him. Jesus does not want followers at any price. He wants disciples who know what they are doing. And so He says: '"Foxes have their holes, the birds their roosts; but the Son of Man has nowhere to lay his head."'[10]

Foxes and birds live a perilous existence, always on the move, always in danger. But they have a place of rest every day. Jesus has just been turned out of one town and now must find somewhere to spend the night. And then tomorrow He will continue to Jerusalem where the cross awaits Him.

Following Jesus means accepting the risk of the

unknown. It may mean even losing one's material possessions in exchange for an unseen and, from the worldly perspective, undefined security.[11]

It is marvellous to be told, 'I'll follow you wherever you go.' But Jesus prefers that His followers know from the outset what awaits them rather than that they be moved by a momentary impules, an emotional or a superficial choice. This man might have to leave his career and his economic security.

Perhaps we will be asked to make sacrifices. Perhaps we have already made some and are regretting having done so. Jesus knows it is hard, and for this reason He warns us. He wants us to follow Him, but only if we have made an honest choice, without blindfolds, with no regrets and without looking back.

The story does not tell us how the scribe responded to the warning. Immediately, it focuses on the second encounter. This time Jesus takes the initiative. He sees someone and says: 'Follow me.'

We do not know what Jesus sees in this unknown face when He invites him to follow. The text says only that the young man responds: '"Let me go and bury my father first."'[12] A praiseworthy request from a good son. Or so it seems. And so Jesus' response seems hard: '"Leave the dead to bury their dead; you must go and announce the kingdom of God."'[13]

What does He mean? In a society where burying a relative is a sacred duty, how can Jesus ask someone to leave his dead father without a burial?[14]

In Palestine funerals took place very soon after the death. In fact, in many instances they took place the same day.[15] That rush was due not only to laws of hygiene and to the hot climate but, also, to religious custom. As long as there was a dead body in a home, everything in that home was considered unclean. Custom also demanded that the son accompany his father's body to the tomb.

If this young man is not at this moment attending to his dead father, it is simply because his father is not dead. The expression 'let me go and bury my father' is really another way of saying, 'Wait until my father dies.' The young man is looking for an excuse to put off a decision. What he is saying is: 'Let me continue to live my life the way I choose. Once I am free from family pressures then I will follow you.'

The young man's father could still be quite young. Many years could pass before the young man found the right moment to accept Jesus' invitation. For this reason, Jesus answers with a sentence which is really packed with spiritual truth: 'Let the dead bury their dead.'

If this young man wished to consecrate his life to God's service he was exempt by law from the responsibility of burying his father. Considering the patriarchal society in which the story occurs, it is most probable that there were other family members who could care for the father, thus leaving the young man free to follow his calling.[16]

Jesus' answer amounts to this: 'I understand your duties as a son. But you are not thinking of a pious act but are looking for a way to postpone your decision until a hypothetical situation occurs. Do not be afraid to place your trust in God and your conscience above your respect for tradition or custom.

'Anyone can bury the dead. Trying to raise men from spiritual death is more difficult. This is what I call you to do. Now that you have found the secret of life, go and tell others. Let those who are spiritually dead entrench themselves behind their pretexts. Do not fight between God's call and worldly pressures any more. Accept life and share it with others. Perhaps you can even start with your own father.'

When conscience speaks, there are no worthy excuses. Procrastination is probably one of our worst enemies. It prevents us from choosing, from acting upon our choices, from living. Jesus calls to us today. He asks us to choose Him, not tomorrow but today.

While Jesus' words still hang in the air, a third person comes near.

' "I will follow you, sir; but let me first say goodbye to my people at home." '

Hearing this irresolute, hesitant promise, Jesus responds:

"'No one who sets his hand to the plough and then keeps looking back is fit for the kingdom of God.'"[17] Is this another insensitive answer? Cannot this man even be allowed to say 'Goodbye' to his family?

In order to understand Jesus' answer, one must remember that to say goodbye to one's family in biblical times meant much more than simply saying 'Goodbye'. Those farewells could last not hours but days and weeks. They could even last months or years.[18] Saying farewell meant separating oneself for good from all family matters. 'Let me go and finish with my affairs' meant 'everything that is part of my life.' It included family members, possible inheritances, successions and business dealings.

Confronted by such fear, Jesus responds by saying that if someone wants to advance he must stop looking behind. Perhaps Jesus could see tidy fields with their furrows running straight and long. Perhaps when He made this statement He could even see a farmer guiding his horse and plough in the distance. Certainly the farmer could never make straight, long furrows by looking backwards over his shoulder.

Family, friends, and business all exert pressure upon us. They have a hold upon us which is difficult to break away from. Jesus may not necessarily be asking us to leave it all behind. But He certainly is asking us to manage these things in the light of our relationship to Him. Such management will require changes. If we are continually thinking of what we leave behind, we may end up as Lot's wife, forever imprisoned by our past.[19]

The story ends without telling us of their final decisions. Did the three follow Jesus? Did any of them follow Him? The Gospel writers choose not to satisfy our curiosity.[20] They simply present us with the three cases and abruptly suggest one question: 'What are you going to do?'

To those of us who, like the intellectual, naïvely promise to follow Christ, Jesus warns us that to follow Him means taking risks.

To those of us who, like the father's cautious and spoiled boy, wish to postpone our decision until later, Jesus warns us of the danger involved in postponing the decision indefinitely.

To those of us who, like the indecisive worker, wait for all our problems to disappear, Jesus reminds us that we cannot follow Him halfway, from a distance, or only now and then.

Jesus knows that we are afraid of such commitment. He does not condemn us for that. Instead, He invites us to test His liberating power.

When we decide to sacrifice everything for Him, we actually allow God to break the threefold chain of fear which holds us back. When we choose to follow Jesus, He frees us from the weight of the past, from the fear of the present, and from the uncertainty of the future.

'Here and now' is the only space in time which we possess. This brief, fleeting moment is our moment of decision. It can be our moment of surrender, complete and without reservations. It can be our moment of freedom.

---

[1] Luke 9:51-53. The hatred between Jews and Samaritans stems from the War of Secession between the sons of Solomon which ended in the separation of the kingdom into Judah and those of the North (1 Kings 12). The political conflict gave rise to a religious conflict which became more acute during the Assyrian reign when the population was forced to mix with the pagan colonists (2 Kings 17). The irreversible division finally occurred at the end of the Babylonian exile when Judah rejected reconciliatory attampts by Samaria along with their help in rebuilding the Temple at Jerusalem. (*Ezra* 4.) The Samaritans built their own temple on Mt. Gerizim. And in the year 108BC the Jews destroyed it. In Jesus' time, the Orthodox treated Samaritans as heretics, legally as impure as the pagans (see Luke 9:51-56; John 4:9; 8:48).

[2] According to Josephus, the trip from Galilee to Jerusalem took at least three days since Samaritan territory was evaded at all costs, (*Life* 269), thus requiring that the traveller go around by the other side of the Jordan. It appears that on some occasions Jesus also used that route, (Matt. 19:1), although the gospels underline His boldness and even His preference for the route which passed directly through Samaria (Luke 9:51-56; John 4:1-5, 39-43). Jesus' lack of prejudice towards the Samaritans was completely unusual (Luke 10:33; 17:16; John 4:5-40). Later, the early church followed His example and made the mission to Samaria an important work (Acts 1:8; 8:5-25; 9:31; 15:3).

[3] Without doubt, one of His teachings most difficult to follow was that of loving one's enemy (Matt. 5:38-41, 43-45) and to find greatness in service (Mark 10:42-45).

[4] Luke 9:54 (NEB).

90 ALONG THE WAY

[5] According to Luke 9:51, this story takes place at the beginning of the long trek up to Jerusalem which would end in the Passover Feast. Jesus would never return to that spot.

[6] Luke 9:55, 56 (NIV).

[7] The violent reaction of the disciples could have been motivated by their fear of sleeping in the open, thus placing themselves at the risk of falling victim to one of the numerous thieving bands and terrorists who circulated through the country (Josephus, *War* 2:228; 1:310-313), which was devastated by unemployment and misery (cf. Matt. 20:1-16).

[8] Luke 9:57-62.

[9] This precision is given by the parallel text of Matt. 8:19.

[10] Luke 9:58 (NEB).

[11] It is curious that, when talking with the scribe, Jesus calls Himself 'Son of man', a title which no one gives Him in the gospels but which He uses with a special preference. This title underscores His humanity and the insecurity and vulnerability which this brings with it. At the same time, it identifies Him as the Messiah, since 'Son of man' is also the term used by the prophet Daniel (7:13, 14) to describe the one who would come to save His own and to restore His Kingdom of peace. With this title, Jesus emphasizes the reality of His submission, His humiliation, and suffering through which, and only through which, He would secure His Kingdom. He is warning this possible disciple that it is not easy to get the glory without first enduring the cross.

[12] Luke 9:59.

[13] Luke 9:60 (NEB).

[14] Jesus severely rebuked those who chose not to obey the commandment to honour their parents (Exod. 20:12), although they did so by using religious excuses (Mark 7:6-13). To Him, it was so important to look after one's parents that He tried to provide the best possible care for His mother, even though He was agonizing and suffering on the cross (John 19:25-27).

[15] See Acts 5:1-10.

[16] Num. 6:1-8. Jesus had to face the misunderstanding of His own family when He chose to follow His mission in life (John 7:1-10; Matt. 12:46-50; Mark 3:31-35; Luke 8:19-21). And He predicted that many of His followers would have to face the same thing. (See Luke 12:51-53 where Jesus paraphrases the prophecy of Micah 7:6.)

[17] Luke 9:61, 61 (NEB).

[18] This surprising fact can be tested by reading the farewells of Judges 19 or those of 1 Kings 19 and 20.

[19] Gen. 19:23-26; Luke 17:28-33.

[20] In reality, the text doesn't end with these three encounters which, without doubt, leave a feeling of failure because who feels more called than these men to follow Christ? The story continues; and shows us that with Divine help what seems impossible by our own capabilities is not only possible, but is exceedingly fruitful. Immediately after these three encounters, Jesus has seventy followers. When He sends these new disciples out to

preach the Gospel, they are well aware that their strength lies not in their virtues or personal qualifications, but in the power of the One who has sent them. 'I am he who sends you.' (Ibid.) The text says that after completing their mission they returned excited (Luke 10:17-24). In order to understand this supreme joy, the next time that Jesus invites us to follow Him, instead of looking for excuses as did the three in our story, we must respond simply:

'Yes, I will follow you. I accept your way, not because I feel I am better than those three but because you are asking me as well. If you, who can see things more clearly, feel that I am worth calling, it is because you know I can serve in some way.'

Under a tree

A shout fills the streets like a summer wind storm. It rushes through the town as an unexpected sea-wind in the afternoon, violently opening windows two by two, calling the women to their thresholds, stopping the men at work, causing the children to run like a herd of young goats through the streets. The name being shouted awakens this sleepy village.

He is here, and everyone is curious. Until now His name has been the topic of backroom conversations, of chatter between neighbours, of private talk in the family room. Today it is in the streets. The name has been heard from Galilee to Decapolis, from Judea to Samaria, from Jerusalem to the Jordan. Today it has come to Jericho.[1]

Preceded by the cloud of dust and children, the rumour moves as a whirlwind through gardens and byways, streets and alleys. With it come expectation, curiosity, and mystery, 'Jesus of Nazareth'. The name passes from one mouth to another. Everyone hopes that He is the Messiah. They place the blind, the lame, the sick, and the mutilated in His path. They bring their paralysed, their demon-possessed, their crazy folk. They lay them down in the street and wait hopefully for Jesus to come.[2]

Jesus stops to talk with those who line the way. He pauses to talk with those who stand at the crossroads of their lives. He spreads images, parables, and stories upon the wind where, like God's first words, He makes a new world appear out of nothing[3] in the hearts of His listeners.

He does not have a title as do the doctors. He does not depend on tradition as do the rabbis and the scribes. He speaks on His own authority, and therein lies His charm. With words thousands of years old He raises people's sights to new horizons and sparks hope where none existed.[4] He awakens their dead hearts to new and exciting destinies.

His words are carried on the wind. Their echoes pass through the streets and plazas, sounding from patios and roof-tops. They even reach inside the vault where the publican Zacchaeus spends the days of his life suffering, swearing and dreaming, as he sits alone, counting his money.

Zacchaeus, chief of the publicans, is rich and powerful.[5] He holds an important government post. Ambition has driven him throughout the years until he has finally reached the top. He had needed to fill the void in his life somehow, to feel important, and he had hoped that his townsmen would finally recognize his attributes and abilities when he had accepted the job.

Rather than gaining their respect, he has gained their hatred and their scorn. They exclude him from the synagogue.[6] They consider him a traitor for his collaboration with the enemy. They jeer at his name which means 'pure' in his language. As if this was not enough, they continually jest about his short stature.

Zacchaeus is rich — and lonely. The fact that he is an oppressor does not change his own feelings of inadequacy. His feelings of loneliness reinforce his feelings of guilt. Ever since his colleague, Matthew of Capernaum, had left his lucrative position in order to follow this new prophet, an obsession to know more about the Teacher has not let Zacchaeus rest. His conscience urges him towards honesty and right.

Zacchaeus needs acceptance, yet he hardly dares to hope for it. What sort of teacher would accept a tax collector into His group of closest friends![7] The law makes it very clear that tax collectors had no rights and deserve no pity.[8] And yet rumour has it that this Teacher has accepted Matthew. Does he dare to hope?

Upon hearing that the Teacher is in Jericho, Zacchaeus hurriedly closes his office and runs out into the streets in his search. If Jesus has been able to change Matthew's life, then perhaps there is hope for him.

Zacchaeus meets a human wall when he steps from his office. It closes in front of him. On other occasions, money would have purchased him a way through the crowd. But, today, the mob will not let him past. Humiliated, Zacchaeus strains, unsuccessfully, to see above the crowd. His small stature does not allow him even a glimpse. But he can hear the cries of the blind man, Bartimaeus: 'Jesus, son of David, have mercy on me.'[9]

This cry echoes painfully in his own wounded heart. Then he hears a voice which asks: 'What do you want me to do for you?'[10]

This is what Zacchaeus has been waiting to hear. But he cannot hear the answer which is drowned by the noise of the crowd screaming for the blind man to receive his sight.

Frustration fills him and he trembles with desire. Just when he is ready to leave, swearing at his bad luck, a crazy idea occurs to him. He runs, afraid to lose this last opportunity. Jesus has just entered Jericho, and while He slowly makes His way through the crowded streets, Zacchaeus leaves the crowds behind. He runs desperately through the empty side-streets until he reaches a neighbourhood on the edge of the city. He knows that Jesus must pass by here on His way out of the city. He threads his way through the familiar alleyways until, turning one last corner, he comes upon it. The old sycamore tree still stands, stretching its branch out over the street. The tree he had climbed so many times as a boy beckons to him once more.

Luke describes the scene.[11] The stiff tax official pants as he hurriedly picks his way through the branches. The crowd approaches. Zacchaeus straddles the old branch. He leans down to see Jesus, but he hopes, more than anything, that no one will look up.

The crowd passes beneath the tree. At last he will be able to see the prophet. His heart misses a beat as the Teacher stops directly under the tree. He watches Jesus touch the sick and he hears Him speak words of comfort to the crowd. Suddenly Jesus stops and looks up into the tree. To Zacchaeus' horror, the crowd does the same. Loud laughter breaks out.

'Look who is up there in the tree!'

Zacchaeus had climbed the tree to find relief from his suffering. Now, red-faced with embarrassment, he knows that he has become the laughing stock of Jericho. But then, Jesus, who is not laughing, looks at him respectfully and, with total naturalness and genius, turns Zacchaeus' ridiculous plight into a triumph. As if talking to a friend, Jesus says: 'Zacchaeus, come down immediately. I have finally arrived. I must stay at your house today.'[12]

Zacchaeus is so surprised he almost falls out of the tree. When he finally reaches the ground, the crowd opens to let him pass. Zacchaeus wonders if he is dreaming when Jesus greets him as a lifelong friend. He cannot believe that the great Teacher accepts him — hated, evil, lonely Zacchaeus. He cannot believe that the Teacher is willing to eat and sleep in his home.

Jesus knows that, if treated with enough respect and love, we each have incredible potential. He comes to Zacchaeus and He comes to us today to show us just how valuable we are to Him. He does not even notice all the trappings which we have accumulated in order to boost our own self-esteem. He comes to our houses today to love us just as we are.

Once at home, far from the crowd, Zacchaeus opens his heart to the Teacher. The Teacher, in turn, helps Zacchaeus to open his heart to God's love. Knowing at last that he is accepted, Zacchaeus no longer needs to hide behind his money and his power. Loved at last, he can now reach out to help others. He no longer needs to step on others in order to raise himself up. He can now take their hands and lift them up to stand with him in brotherhood.

All at once, Zacchaeus feels pity for those whose misery he has helped to cause. He feels forgiveness towards those who laughed at him. Suddenly he sees others not as people to be exploited but as brothers.

While the crowd in the street murmur against the impious publican and the Teacher who has decided to stay with him, Zacchaeus and Jesus make plans to help them.[13] The riches accumulated at the expense of others no longer makes Zacchaeus happy. He does not want them. He decides to give half to the poor. And, to those whom he has defrauded, he chooses to repay four times over.[14] His encounter with Jesus has shown him the joy of giving.

We all suffer, like Zacchaeus, from our choices of expediency which separate us from our fellow men. We all live in various degrees of loneliness behind closed doors. Perhaps we have engineered a promotion by stepping on others in order to get it. Or maybe we work long hours in order to provide those extras which will place us just that little bit above our neighbours. By trying to boost our own self-esteem we alienate the very friends we need. As we sit alone counting our treasures and our titles, Jesus' words break in upon our silent loneliness and challenge us to unlock those doors.

Jesus offers His acceptance to us today. He comes to return to us our hope and our enthusiasm for the good and the noble. We live in a world where destruction and discouragement reign. But Jesus offers us a love, powerful enough to pull down our wall of fear. His love will enable us to reach out to others. Rather than seeing others as our competitors or our enemies, we shall see them as candidates for eternal life who need acceptance as much as we do.

The love of Jesus gives us the strength necessary to give what we have in service. When we accept His love for us, our lives become irresistible sources of power. Following Him means more than sympathizing with Christian ideology. Anyone who is really committed to heavenly things must be committed to helping here below.

Jesus comes to us today, as He did to Zacchaeus, offering His love and acceptance. He invites us to leave our struggle after economic power and social triumph and to join Him in service. He invites us to open our hearts in generosity. He invites us to stop manipulating or utilizing others for our own selfish motives. He invites us to decide against injustice and to work to abolish its causes. He calls us to be lights in a world of darkness.[15]

If we find it difficult to share our money, our time, or our faith, it means that we are in need of an encounter with Jesus. Only He can open our eyes to the depths of His love and to the depths of human need.

---

[1] Luke places this story chronologically as the last public ministry of Jesus outside Jerusalem, just before Holy Week (Luke 19:1-10).

[2] The people expected the Messiah's arrival to bring with it solutions for

all evil. He would come to 'bring good news to those who suffer, to heal the broken hearts, to proclaim pardon for the captives and liberty for those in prison . . . to console the afflicted . . . to change . . . their . . . mourning to celebration and their low spirits into songs.' (Isa. 61:1-3; Luke 4:16-21; 7:18-22.)

[3] John 6:60-68.

[4] Luke 1:78, 79. The messianic hope was made up of the following ideas (*Exodus Rabbah* 25:21): 'The only Holy One, blessed be, will restore ten things in the new world: (1) He will illuminate the world with His light . . . and on any who are sick He will cause the sun to shine in order to cure them, as it is written: "But for you who repeat my Name the Sun of Justice will be born and His wings will bring health." (Mal. 4:2). (2) He will cause a well to spring up in Jerusalem and anyone who suffers pain will find health there as it is written: "It will bring health. Where this water flows everything will live." (Ezek. 47:9). (3) He will cause the trees to bear fruit each month and all who eat of their fruit will be healed, as it is written: "Each month it will give new fruit . . . and its fruit will serve as food and its leaves as medicine." (Ezek. 47:12). (4) All the cities which were destroyed will be rebuilt . . . as it is written: "And your sisters, Sodom and her daughters . . . will return to their first state." (Ezek. 16:55). (5) Jerusalem will be rebuilt with precious stones, as it is written: "I will make your stones sapphires. Your battlements will be made of rubies, your gates of emeralds, and your walls of precious stones." (Isa. 54:11, 12). (6) Peace will reign in nature, as it is written: "The wolf will lie with the lamb." (Isa. 11:6-9). (7) God will make a new covenant between men and animals, as it is written: "That day I will make for you a covenant with the savage beasts, with the birds of the air, and with the reptiles of the ground." (Hos. 2:(18) 20). (8) He will end all suffering in the world, as it is written: "You will not hear screams or cries." (Isa. 65:19). (9) Death will cease to exist, as it is written: "He will destroy death forever." (Isa. 25:8). (10) And happiness will reign forever as it is written: "They will come to Zion with singing upon their heads forever." (Isa. 35:10).

[5] Luke 19:2.

[6] Anyone who accepted a position as a tax collector was expelled from the community and he could not be reaccepted unless he gave up his career (*Tos. Demai* 3:4). Those who held such jobs were considered equal to slaves (*Rosh ha-Shanah* 1:8), and their word had no value, not even as testimony (*Sanhedrin* 3:3). If tax collectors fell into a pit 'They should not be pulled out, neither should pagans or pig-herders.' (*Tos. Baba Metzi'a* 2:33.) Perhaps this helps us to understand the boldness which Jesus exhibited in permitting a publican to become a disciple. (Matt. 9:9; 10:3.)

[7] Matt. 9:9-13; Mark 2:13-17; cf. Matt. 10:14; Mark 3:13-19; Luke 6:12-16.

[8] Tax collectors, money-brokers, and publicans were included in the list of thieves and criminals (*Nedarim* 3:4).

[9] Luke places the healing of the blind man 'as Jesus entered into Jericho' (Luke 18:35-43), and the story of Zacchaeus 'as He passed through the city'

(Luke 19:1). The name Bartimaeus is given in Mark 10:46-52 (cf. Matt. 20:29-34).

[10] Mark 10:51.
[11] Luke 19:2-4.
[12] Luke 19:5.
[13] Luke 19:7-10.
[14] Rabbinical writings prohibited a person dedicating more than a fifth of their wealth to the poor (j *Pesahim* 1:1, 15 b). Wills that exceeded that amount were not considered legal, since it was considered a religious duty to reserve enough for their retirement. Zacchaeus' decision to give half of his wealth to the poor, thus compensating abundantly for any suffering caused (Luke 19:8) was, in itself, a large transgression against the pious writings.
[15] Matt. 5:13-16.

At the feast

The monotonous routine of the city has been swept aside by a dizzy excitement which invades everything. It is the Great Feast,[1] and it brings new faces and fresh ideas to Jerusalem.

The euphoria of Passover accompanies the arrival of spring.[2] The smell of flowers and fresh grass floats on the air. Life springs forth, welcomed by the sun. It vibrates in the sounds of new birth. It flows in the sap which dresses the trees in bright new foliage. It fills people with new hope and makes the heart beat faster. The feast exudes happiness. The old cherish again the innocence of youth. The noise of adolescence and the games of childhood fill the market-places and squares.

But celebrations are also times of memory and nostalgia, and the Passover is no exception. It is Israel's most important feast. It commemorates the flight from Egypt when Israel gained her national independence. When night falls, family and friends recline around the festive table to remember this historic moment. They eat the symbolic lamb with bitter herbs. They drink abundantly from the cup of the blessing. Together they sing the traditional Psalms which praise God, the Saviour who led their nation from slavery to freedom.[3]

Somewhere between piety and pride, the true meaning of the Passover can be found. It signifies the Divine election of Israel as the chosen people of God. It commemorates the night when God saved a multitude of prisoners. It reminds the people of the final liberation which will come with the arrival of the Messiah.[4] The Passover is the great melting pot of all Israel's expectations, promises, and hopes.[5]

Thousands of visitors crowd into Jerusalem. There are pilgrims, travelling salesmen, beggars, and foreigners[6] — Israelites who had been scattered in the Dispersion return to the Holy City for the Passover. Heathen worshippers looking for something new in the spiritual rituals of Judaism also come to this, its biggest festival. Among these pagans are a group of Greeks — and they are looking for Jesus.[7]

They do not look for Jesus in the dark austerity of a cloister or in the bleak confines of a monastery. They look for Him among the crowds, interacting with humanity.

Too often we believe that spirituality can be found only in solitude, abstinence, solemnity and tedium. We forget that Jesus is the very essence of freedom, plenty, happiness, and personal fulfilment.[8]

The Greeks find Jesus at the Feast. They do not know that His mission on earth is drawing rapidly to a close with His coming death. They know only that He has just entered Jerusalem as the Messiah,[9] and they come looking for Him. They sense that an interview with Jesus will be of more interest to them than the Temple ceremonies. They are dissatisfied with their own cultural philosophy and are no longer impressed by the liturgy of Israel. Intelligent and sensitive, these Greeks look for something that will quench their spiritual thirst. They come to Jesus, wanting to discover Him for themselves.

Their first contact is with Philip, a disciple from Bethsaida of Galilee. Bethsaida has been influenced greatly by Greek culture. Unlike the other disciples, who bear good Hebrew or Aramaic names, Philip bears a Greek name which is a silent testimony to the Hellenistic influence on his parents.[10] The Greeks approach Him because he understands their language.

'We would like to see Jesus.'[11]

Philip is a bit disconcerted by these, the first foreigners to take an interest in Jesus. Not knowing what to do, he takes them to Andrew. Andrew, who also bears a Greek name, is the older and wiser one.[12]

Even among the people of our secular, post-Christian world, there are many who wish to know Jesus. Like the Greeks, they have heard of Him, and they wish to see Him for themselves. What is more, they would like to find Him in us.

With questions less direct than the one addressed to Philip, they also turn to us, the Philips and Andrews of today.

Human personality is essentially projective. What we are, what we think, what we feel, and what we believe is, in one form or other, projected on to what we do. Earlier or later, it will show its face in our words or attitudes or even in our silences. The Bible describes it in this way: '"For the words that the mouth utters come from the overflowing of the heart."'[13] It is impossible to hide our beliefs in our every-day living. And although it is true that the 'cowl does not make the monk', the monk does choose to wear the robe or cowl of the order of which he is a member. Others identify us by the image we unknowingly (or knowingly) project.

If we are Christians what others see in us affects their concept of Christianity. They come looking for Jesus. What do they really see? Do they see Christ in us?

For some, taking care of their image means putting on a mask[14] once in a while, whenever it is convenient, in some sort of personal charade. They value their reputations, even if they misrepresent their true characters. But the important thing is what is underneath. God created us 'in His image'.[15] His desire is that we 'should be shaped to the likeness of His Son'.[16] That is, that we allow Him to touch us so deeply that looking to Jesus, we become like Him.

Paul, with his great practical psychology, says that we reflect what we study: 'Because for us there is no veil over the face, we all reflect as in a mirror the splendour of the Lord; thus we are transfigured into His likeness, from splendour to splendour; such is the influence of the Lord who is Spirit.'[17]

If we do not reflect Christ, it is because we do not look at Him. And if we reflect Him badly, it can only be because we do not look at Him with keen perception. As a cracked mirror, we too are in danger of distorting into a grotesque caricature the image of God.

The normal process which God expects in our spiritual lives is that we continue reflecting, each time more transparently, His character. Since we become what we study, what ultimately happens is that our images do not change but our characters do. Instead of trying to imitate the external aspects of Christianity, it is wiser to allow ourselves to be transformed from within.

Jesus says: '"I am the vine, and you the branches. He who dwells in me, as I dwell in him, bears much fruit; for apart from me you can do nothing. . . . No branch can bear fruit by itself, but only if it remains united with the vine; no more can you bear fruit, unless you remain united with me."'[18]

One who really depends on the vine does not need to take care of his image. In time, the fruits will come. Others will see them and will desire to enjoy this dependency on the vine themselves. Setting oneself up as a good example falls far short of displaying in one's life the fruits of the Spirit.

The relationship between a true believer and God is, in a certain sense, like that of a light bulb and the electrical connection. When contact is made, the light bulb shines automatically.

Andrew and Philip are unsure of what to do; but, ultimately, as friends of Jesus they do what is necessary. They lead the Greeks to Him.

These Greeks who come to see Jesus bring Him great satisfaction: They are the evidence that His work has not been in vain.[19] Impelled by their spiritual hunger, they find in Him what they have been looking for outside their own culture and religion. Perhaps for this reason He says to them: '"The hour has come for the Son of Man to be glorified."'[20] The time has come when He should be worshipped and acknowledged as the Christ.

Jesus waits for us to bring others to Him today as he did Philip and Andrew. The time is here when He should be worshipped and acknowledged as the Son of God. Those who are looking for Him should be able to find Him, not in spite of us but because of us.

In His conversation with the Greeks, Jesus refers to the phenomena occurring in nature whereby seemingly dead plants produce life.[21] He compares each human being to a grain of wheat: '"In truth, in very truth I tell you, a grain of wheat remains a solitary grain unless it falls into the ground and dies; but if it dies, it bears a rich harvest.'"[22]

Sometimes we are dry and barren, simply because we depend too much upon ourselves. We are like seeds in storage. We try to exist without the universal fountain of life. If we would bury ourselves in the furrows of our needy world, divine vitality would force its way out of us and nothing could stop its germination. If we would allow ourselves to fall into the good ground, our roots would grow deep. And one day, from that small, insignificant grain, divine flowers would grow into incredible fruit.

Jesus adds a surprising statement: '"The man who loves his life will lose it, while the man who hates his life in this world will keep it for eternal life."'[23]

It is simply a matter of choice. In order to germinate and perpetuate, we must die to our lives and allow life itself to break in and to grow within us.[24] Only then, as believers, can we finally stop worrying about our image. Only then will the Greeks of our day see Jesus in us.[25]

---

[1] From the time that the kings centralized the worship at Jerusalem, the Passover lost its family emphasis and became a celebration in the city of which all were obliged to attend. (Reform of Josiah in 621BC, 2 Kings 23:1-25). Except for the small temple at Onias in Leontopolis (from 170BC to AD73), the Temple at Jerusalem was the only Jewish sanctuary in the world. Pilgrims the world over came to Jerusalem to worship three times a year, and brought to the city a large amount of revenue and trade, since they were expected to bring their tithes and offerings. (Shekalim 7:2.)

[2] The Feast of the Passover began on the evening of the 14th day of Nisan (April), the last day before the full moon which followed the spring equinox. It lasted seven days, which were called 'days of unleavened bread' because during that time no one could eat leavened bread or use or even have at home any yeast or fermented thing (Exod. 12:5-20. cf Pesahim 3:1).

[3] Exod. 12:1-28. The sacrifice of the lamb was performed in the Temple in groups of more than ten people and fewer than twenty. Each father of a family or head of a group had personally to cut the throat of the lamb in front of the altar in the presence of a priest, while a choir of Levites sang the Hallel (Ps. 113 to 118). After sunset, each group united in Jerusalem for the Passover supper. (Pesahim 10:1-4.) The supper followed a ritual pattern called Seder which has changed little throughout the centuries. The participants rested upon rugs or couches around a low table, imitating the customs of the wealthy. The ceremony began with the blessing by the head of the family, offered over the first of four cups of wine which would be

drunk throughout the supper. The wine had to be red and mixed with hot water, without doubt to imitate the blood of the passover lamb. (*Pesahim* 7:13.) The meal began with a salad of lettuce, turnips and other 'bitter herbs', which was dipped in water mixed with salt or vinegar to represent the sweat and tears of slavery. The lamb was served whole, without a broken bone, (John 19:33) and was eaten with unleavened bread. The high point was the rite of the Haggada, when the youngest child asked his father to explain each piece used in the ritual and then they sang the first part of the Hallel (Ps. 113 and 114; *Pesahim* 9:3; 10:3-4). After the second cup the father blessed the bread and served it before serving the lamb. The bread was dipped at least once in a thick sauce which was called 'haroseth' (*Pesahim* 2:6) a type of apple sauce mixed with figs and grapes with pieces of cinnamon sticks, which, by its colour and consistency represented the clay and the straw with which their ancestors made the bricks in Egypt. (Exod. 5:5-18.) The ceremony ended after the third cup, called the 'blessing' or 'the redemption' with the singing of the great Hallel (Ps. 114-118). The rest of the night was to be spent in meditation and prayer (*Pesahim* 10:8 a).

⁴The name 'Passover' (in Hebrew *Pesah*) was associated with the action of 'passing overhead' or 'passing in front of' and commemorated the night when God 'passed over the houses of the children of Israel in Egypt' and freed their ancestors (Exod. 12:13, 23, 27). The term seems to mean 'passing over in protection' as the Mekilta by Rabbi Yismael (Citing Isa. 31:5) states: 'As the hen covers her young with her wings so Jehovah will save Jerusalem from the armies. He will save her and free her; protect her and preserve her.' Salvation was the central theme of this feast as is demonstrated by the main prayer of the ceremony; 'We give thanks to God who has done marvellous things with our fathers and with us. He has brought us from slavery to freedom . . . from servanthood to salvation.' (*Pesahim* 10:5, 6.) According to *Midrash Mekilta* on Exodus 12:42: 'The night of Passover has been fixed for the salvation of all generations of Israel.' This belief was carried so far that they believed that the Messianic salvation would come on a night during Passover: 'In that night we were saved and in another like it we will be saved.' (*Targum* on Exod. 12:1, according to manuscript 110 of Paris.)

⁵According to 'the song of the four nights' (See Roger le Deaut, *La nuit pascale — Essai sur la signification de la paque juive a partir du Targum d'Exod XII:42*, Instituto Biblico, Rome, 1980, pages 4-65) the Passover celebrated God's four most important interventions on this earth: (1) The night of the creation of light at the beginning of the world; (2) The night of the covenant with Abraham at the beginning of the Hebrew history; (3) The night of the Exodus, at the beginning of the Hebrew history as a free nation; (4) The night of the coming of the Messiah when He would finally establish the kingdom of God.

⁶During the Passover, between 100,000 and 200,000 pilgrims arrived at Jerusalem and stayed at least eight to fifteen days. These visitors far outnumbered the townsmen. The pilgrims' stay was necessarily prolonged to more than a week, because in order to go to the Temple those who came

from pagan countries had to go through seven days of a purifying ritual (*Jubilees* 49:2, 6).

⁷According to the religious law of the day, all Jews were obliged to attend the three main feasts in the Temple, except for: 'the deaf, the idiot, the minor, those of doubtful sex, women, unfreed slaves, the malformed, the blind, the sick, the old, and all those who could not walk up the mountain of the Temple.' (*Hagigah* 1:1.) In practice, those who lived too far away were obligated only to attend once a year. (*Pesahim* 9.) Philo says that 'many come to each Feast, some by land, others by sea, from the east and west, the north and south.' (*De specialibus legibus* 1:12.) Proselytes were obliged only to come to the feasts if they were circumcised (cf. Gal. 5:3). We have many testimonies of foreign unbelievers who were drawn to Jerusalem by the magnetic power of her religious festivals (*War* 6:9, 3). According to Josephus, among those in Jerusalem during the Passover of the year 70 were 2,000 foreigners (*Life* 65:354).

⁸I think that it is interesting to observe that during His ministry Jesus did not oblige His disciples to fast (Matt. 9:14, 15; Mark 2:18-20; Luke 5:33-35), considering that fasting was a popular religious practice during His day, not only for the pious Pharisees but even among the disciples of John the Baptist. Jesus meant for His teachings to be the way to find true happiness: 'I have taught you all these things so that you may have My joy and so that your joy may be complete.' (John 15:11.)

⁹Jesus' triumphal entry into Jerusalem is the last event recorded by John before the incident with the Greeks (John 12:12-19).

¹⁰Philip means 'friend of horses'. Normally, Israelites gave Hebrew names to their children. These generally were related to God in some way: the other disciples had names such as Simon — 'he who listens to God', James — 'God protects', Matthew — 'man of God', John — 'God has given His grace', Judas — 'praised by the Lord', etc. In the Greek-Roman times the Jews of the Dispersion often carried a second Greek or Latin name. For example, Saul of Tarsus used the Latin name Paul (Paulus) which means 'small' (Acts 13:9).

¹¹This encounter is told in John 12:20-26.

¹²Andrew means 'male'. Andrew is the second disciple named in two lists of the twelve (Matt. 10:2; Luke 6:14).

¹³Luke 6:45 (NEB).

¹⁴In the Greek and Etruscan theatres the actors wore masks which identified them with stereotypes and which, at the same time, served as amplifiers as they contained a funnel-shaped interior mouthpiece which helped project the sound. Although the theatrical acoustics were excellent, actors still needed to speak up in order to be heard. When the Romans adopted the ancient theatre, they called the masks per-sona, that is, something that serves for sound. The word 'persona' referred primarily to the mask and secondarily it referred to the actor who used the mask; in the end, the characters ended up being called 'persona'. Surprisingly, this word became generalized outside the theatre and eventually became used for any human being. Today, all individuals are called persons. The etymological roots of

106   AT THE FEAST

this word illustrate an important lesson. In real life this transfer also takes place and one tends to be converted into the mask which one most uses. One adopts the image which one has chosen to project until one finally identifies oneself with it. (See Oscar Bloch and Walther Von Warburg — *Dictionnaire etymologique de la langue francaise*, Presses Universitaires de France, Paris, 1968, page 478.)

[15] Gen. 1:26, 27.
[16] Rom. 8:28, 29 (NEB).
[17] 2 Cor. 3:17, 18 (NEB).
[18] John 15:5, 4 (NEB).

[19] One of Israel's expectations was that when the Messiah came, all the nations would come to Zion to be taught by them (Isa. 2:2-5; 56:7; 60:3; Mic. 4:2; *Tobia* 13:13). With these Greeks this beautiful prophecy began to be fulfilled. They were the first-fruits of the universal influence that Jesus would have.

[20] John 12:23 (NEB). The verb used (glorify) comes from *doxa*, which in Greek means 'opinion'. In the Bible it also means 'reputation', 'splendour', and ordinarily 'what establishes fame and gives weight' (the Hebrew root implies the idea of weight, cf. 2 Sam. 14:26). From there the sense of 'social importance' (1 Kings 3:13). To give glory to someone is to recognize his value (or spread it) publicly (Luke 2:14; 19:38; Rev. 4:9; Ps. 3:3; Isa. 42:8, 12).

[21] Francois Mauriac, *Vie de Jesus*, (Flammarion, Paris, 1936) page 217.
[22] John 12:24 (NEB).
[23] John 12:25 (NIV). Literally 'for eternal life'. Present life is the only opportunity we have to make our calling and election sure.
[24] John 12:26.
[25] Acts 4:13.

At a supper

The full moon lights up this clean spring night. Its rays shine down upon the table which is set and ready for the guests. In its cool, clear light, the items on the table take on a distinct form, more real and more meaningful. The breaking of the bread assumes solemn significance. The wine takes on a blood-red appearance.[1]

All are quiet at this strange supper. The disciples do not know that this is the last time they will be together, and Jesus' strange behaviour unnerves them. He prolongs the dinner, with confidences and pauses, hanging upon the intimacy of this special occasion. The disciples have never felt so afraid of separation. They have never before appreciated the company of the one whom, now for the first time, they fear to lose.

Jesus looks around and unexpectedly says: 'The hand of him who is going to betray me is with mine on the table.'[2]

A shiver runs through the group as each examines his own hands.

The hands of Nathanael are frank, simple, and accustomed to being folded in prayer. These hands were folded in prayer the first time that Jesus saw him under the fig tree.[3]

The hands of Andrew are strong, calloused, worn by the sun and the sea. These active hands belong to a seaman.[4] They want to help wherever and whenever help is needed, either distributing bread to the 5,000 or bringing others to Christ.[5]

John's young hands[6] are active, sensitive, and unhardened by life. Jesus looks lovingly upon them, as they move nervously by His side.[7] They are hands which will still make many mistakes. However, in the end, purified by John's love for his Master, his hands will be dedicated to the Gospel of truth and love.[8]

The hands of James are rough, but have character.[9] They are firmly closed in a fist upon the table. These are the hands of an ambitious man who wants so fiercely to hold on to the blessings of God that he dares to claim a privileged seat next to God's throne;[10] courageous hands of the first Apostle to be martyred,[11] who knows from experience that the kingdom of Heaven can be won only by the valiant.[12]

And now we come to the hands of Matthew. They are the hands of a writer, an intellectual, and a banker.[13] Fine and clean, they are able hands. Accustomed to count money, to keep accurate records, these hands will leave the cash-box to take up the pen and write the longest gospel.[14] They are the hands of one who consecrated his talents to Jesus at the Master's bidding. They are the hands of one who dares to say, 'Yes'.

Then we see the hands of Peter. Worn, knotted, and hardened by work, these hands are dedicated to supporting a wife and family.[15] They are impulsive, eager to threaten, and willing to hit back hard.[16] And yet, these hands will gesticulate shamefully in order to deny Jesus.[17] But they are hands which will later be washed in tears of repentance. One day these hands will be nailed to another cross in service to their Master.[18]

Look at the hands . . . .

Simon, what are your hands like? Some call him 'zealot' which means terrorist.[19] Is it possible that there are hands of a terrorist at the Lord's table? Have those hands killed someone? Others call him 'the Cananite' which means patriot or partisan.[20] His are the hands of someone who could be a national hero, but who has chosen to be in God's army. They are hands which will be faithful to their principles to the end.

Then we see the hands of Philip, cosmopolitan and sophisticated. He is the one with connections, the one to whom people turn when they need to meet someone important. When needed, he serves as interpreter for the foreigners who look for Jesus.[21] However, his hands are ones which, at the time of deciding, doubt their usefulness and tremble in the face of action.[22] These hands know how to handle people, yet they tremble when someone comes looking for spiritual help.[23] They belong to a man who wanted to know God[24] and who discovered Him in Jesus.

Now we see the hands of Thaddaeus, a disciple of whom we know very little.[25] What we do know, however, says a lot in favour of his open spirit and of his desire that Jesus be known not only by a small enclosed circle of believers, but by the whole world.[26] His hands are extended in a cordial and brotherly welcome of acceptance. They do not wish to outline a plan of action but to share Jesus with all who come near.

James, son of Alphaeus, is next. This is a disciple of whom we know nothing except his name.[27] His hands, unremarkable and average, will not make history. They are hands which pass unseen; hands which nobody remembers. These hands will complete their modest labour without recognition but probably not without pain. Christ loves these hands as much as all the others.

The hands of Thomas are almost identical to those of his twin.[28] However, they set out in search of a different destiny. They are energetic hands with violent tendencies which act out of conviction but which are difficult to convince. Firm hands, but they are almost pessimistic. Their owner is willing to die for Jesus, but finds it difficult to serve Him.[29] These hands more easily accept defeat than success. They react sceptically, cuttingly, even negatively.[30] They belong to one who is not always present with the group. They belong to one who leaves whenever he pleases. These hands are absent when the others receive the news of the resurrection.[31] Distrustful hands, they must touch in order to believe and must feel in order to accept. These hands will be forced to touch the open wounds in Jesus' side and, through this painful experience, will hold firmly on to those of Jesus, accepting Him as Lord.[32]

'The hand which will betray me is here at the table.' A hand like all the rest, it does not appear more false or more treacherous than the others.[33] It does not appear to belong to a thief.[34] No one would say that it belongs to a criminal.[35] No one would believe that it could be suicidal.[36] No one would believe that this hand is capable of selling a friend for so little.[37]

It is the hand of Judas Iscariot. Would his hands have seemed any different from ours on that moonlit night so full of tragedy and love? Do our hands have anything in common with his? Have ours never committed treason against Jesus, even a little? Do 'the hands which will deny me' include yours and mine?

What do our hands look like? Whose do they resemble? Are they like those of Thomas, Philip, or John? Perhaps they could never be as aggressive as Simon's and maybe they have not defrauded so much as Matthew's. They may not be so anxious to deny with oaths as Peter's. And then again, they may be cast in the same mould.

It does not matter what they have been or what they are. It does not matter if they are young or old, manicured or rough, clean or dirty. Strong or weak, able or clumsy, they are here, invited by Jesus to His supper.

We look upon the hands of Jesus. They are the strong hands of a labourer.[38] Hardened by out-of-doors work, they have had black nails, cuts from the saw and axe, and blows from the hammer.

They are courageous hands which dare to touch the sores of the lepers. They lovingly leave the preaching to one side in order to caress babies and to hold the children. They grasp those of the dead and bring them back to life. They are firm hands which offer rest to the tired and weary.[39]

These generous hands have washed the feet of the disciples and served them supper. Soon they will be nailed to a cross and torn by human cruelty.

Next to Jesus' hands, ours appear infinitely unworthy. And yet Jesus extends His loving hands towards ours,[40] promising us that as long as we remain united to Him, He will transform our hands until they become like His.

---

[1] Text based on Matt. 26:17-35; Mark 14:12-26; Luke 22:7-30; John 13:1-38.

[2] Luke 22:21, 22 (NIV); cf. Matt. 26:20-23; Mark 14:18-21.

[3] John 1:45-51. Comparing the lists given by the disciples themselves (Matt. 10:2-4; Mark 3:16-19; Luke 6:14-16 and Acts 1:13) we can identify Nathanael with Bartholomew (which means 'son of Tolomew').

[4] Andrew was from Bethsaida (John 1:44), brother of Simon Peter (Matt. 4:18) and also a fisherman (Mark 1:16).

⁵See John 6:8, 9; 12:22.

⁶John was a son of Zebedee and James's younger brother (Matt. 4:21; Mark 3:17; Luke 9:54). According to tradition (Eusebius, *Historia ecclesiastica* V, 8:4), he was the youngest of the apostles and the disciple whom Jesus loved (John 13:23; 19:26; 20:2). His action, for example, in beating Peter to the empty grave (John 20:1-10), and in expressing openly his love for Jesus by leaning on Him (John 13:23) seems to confirm his youth.

⁷John 13:23.

⁸Although the question has been debated, John the apostle is thought to be the author of the fourth gospel, of three epistles, and the writer of Revelation (Ireneus, *Adversus Haereses III*, 1:1).

⁹James was a son of Zebedee and a wealthy fisherman, since he had workers in his service (Mark 1:19, 20). He was the older brother of John and along with him was called 'the son of thunder' by Jesus. (Mark 3:17; Luke 9:54.)

¹⁰Matt. 20:20-28; Mark 10:35-45.

¹¹He died, decapitated in the reign of Herod Agrippa I between the years AD41 and 44 (Acts 12:1, 2).

¹²Matt. 11:12 (RVR 77 notes: 'The kingdom of heaven is opened by force and the forced ones will overpower him.')

¹³In his own gospel he calls himself a 'publican', that is, a tax collector (Matt. 10:3).

¹⁴Only Matthew identifies himself as a publican called by Jesus (Matt. 9:9-13). The other gospel writers speak of Levi (Mark 2:13-17; Luke 5:27-32), perhaps to protect the reputation of their co-disciple, not openly identifying a past so difficult to accept in that climate.

¹⁵Peter was from Bethsaida (John 1:44) but lived in Capernaum (Mark 1:21, 29-31), and his mother-in-law lived there with him (cf. Luke 4:38, 39). Paul mentions Peter's wife (1 Cor. 9:5: 'Do we not have the right to be accompanied by a wife, as the other apostles and brothers of the Lord and Cephas?' (RSV.)

¹⁶John 18:10, 11 (cf. Mark 14:43-50; Matt. 26:51-56; Luke 22:47-53).

¹⁷Matt. 26:69-75; Mark 14:66-72; Luke 22:54-62; John 18:25-27.

¹⁸According to tradition, Peter was taken prisoner in the year AD67 during the persecution ordered by Nero (*Quo Vadis?*) and crucified head downward since he considered himself unworthy to die in the same way as had his Lord (Clement of Rome, *Corinthians* 5:7).

¹⁹Luke 6:15; Acts 1:13.

²⁰Matt. 10:4; Mark 3:18. The Aramaic word 'cananite' or 'cananist' doesn't mean 'to be from Cana' but 'full of jealousy' or a 'nationalist and Zealot'.

²¹John 12:21.

²²John 6:5-7.

²³John 12:22.

²⁴John 14:8-10.

²⁵Luke (6:16) says that he was a brother to James. Mark (3:18) calls him Thaddaeus; Matthew (10:3) also calls him Lebbaeus.

[26] John 14:22.

[27] Matt. 10:3; Mark 3:18; Luke 6:15; Acts 1:13.

[28] Thomas comes from the Hebrew *To'am* which, like the Greek *Didimo*, means 'twin' (Matt. 10:3; Mark 3:18; Luke 6:15; Acts 1:13).

[29] John 11:16.

[30] John 14:5.

[31] John 20:24.

[32] John 20:24-29.

[33] Besides the term 'sicarius' or 'the one from Kerioth', the Aramaic word *Ishqurya* which some associate with Iscarioth, meant 'the false one' (Xavier Leon-Dufour, *Dictionnaire du Nouveau Testament*, (Seuil, Paris, 1975), page 269). In all the apostles' lists he is cited last and with the note that he betrayed Jesus (Matt. 10:4; Mark 3:19; Luke 6:16). For more about the denial of Judas, see Matt. 26:14-16, 25; Mark 14:10, 11; Luke 22:36.

[34] John 12:1-6.

[35] The crime of Judas is associated in the gospels with the action of Satan (Luke 22:3; John 6:70, 71; 13:2, 26, 27).

[36] Matt. 27:3-10; Acts 1:18.

[37] Matt. 26:15. Thirty shekels was the price which was paid as the value of a dead slave (Exod. 21:32, cf. Zech. 11:12, 13). The Bible says that this money was used to buy the 'potter's field', since then called Aceldama (field of blood) to be used as a cemetery for foreigners (Acts 1:16-20; Matt. 27:3-10).

[38] Mark 6:3 calls Jesus 'tekton', a Greek term from which the word 'architect' comes and which was translated incorrectly for 'carpenter'. In reality it meant artisan, one who worked in construction — not only in woodwork but also in stone and even metal.

[39] Matt. 11:28-30.

[40] Heb. 7:24, 25; Rom. 8:34.

Under the columns

He has tried to gain time, but the rising tension means that he must now decide. The innocence of the prisoner is clear enough. However, the way things are sizing up, releasing Him could be politically suicidal. Pilate's reputation and even his position could be at stake.

On the other hand, giving in to the pressure of this mob disgusts him. He knows they are lying, and he knows that they are using him. He does not like it, but he has run out of options. Either he pronounces judgement in favour of the accused or he abandons Him to the mercy of the crowd.[1] He can no longer postpone the decision. He must pass judgement on Jesus. But can he manage to make his own escape in the process?[2]

Exasperated by the accusers' insistence and by his own inability to resolve such an unimportant issue, Pilate finds himself at a loss for words. Not knowing what else to ask this strange man whose words he does not understand, he tries one more trick. If only he might declare the prisoner insane, he could then set Him free. Instead of appearing weak, he would be seen to be both just and merciful. In order for his plan to work, he needs the prisoner to make some illogical statement.

Playing upon the prisoner's crazy ideas, Pilate asks: 'Are you the king of the Jews?'[3]

But the prisoner answers: 'Do you say this of your own accord, or because they are pressuring you?'

This man is very sane. He has seen through Pilate's manoeuvring and can see the predicament that the ruler is in. Irritated by the prisoner's discernment and humiliated at the thought of having allowed himself to be trapped in a dispute among fanatics, Pilate snaps back: 'It was your people and your chief priests who handed you over to me. Do you not hear how many things they are accusing you of?'[4]

The high priest has already pronounced the death sentence. However, he does not have the power to execute it.

He needs the governing powers to sanction his ruling and for this reason the Roman procurator is consulted.[5]

The prosecution is composed of members of the Sanhedrin, the official representatives of the most deep-rooted religion of the land. For reasons which the procurator will soon discover, these religious leaders are inciting the crowd to ask for the crucifixion of a man whose only crime has been to open the country's eyes to the failure of their spiritual leaders and to preach a more brotherly and genuine faith.[6]

They condemn Him to death because He condemns their lives.[7] Many of those present can repeat from memory His revolutionary words: 'Love your enemies. Do good to those who despise you. Bless those who curse you. Pray for those who hurt you and persecute you.'[8]

Pilate returns to the questioning: 'So, do you claim to be a king or not?'

Jesus looks directly at him and says: 'It is true that I want to reign, but in a different way. If my kingdom was like all the others, I would have had soldiers to fight for me. My mission is to bring truth to the world. He who is in favour of the truth listens to me.'[9]

The truth? Pilate glances at Jesus' hands which are swollen by the thick cords that bind them together at the wrists. How can a man in this situation advocate 'Truth'? Pilate cannot understand why the prisoner refuses to defend Himself against His accusers in order to save His own skin. Who cares about the truth? Voicing his thoughts, Pilate asks the question: 'What is truth?'[10]

Every human being asks the question at least once. Yet few men have the opportunity personally to direct the question at the only One who knows the answer. Pilate does not realize that this opportunity is his. His reaction is one of a sceptic. He pretends to profess an official faith in the empire and in the emperor only out of political expediency.[11] In reality, he believes in nothing.

Pilate asks about truth with indifference, not expecting an answer. He shows all of the conceited flippancy of a worldly man and all the short-sighted cleverness of a politician who puts his faith in the power of force, of mighty rulers and empires.[12]

Looking condescendingly upon the defendant from his position as a high government official he proposes a compromise. Hoping to end the trial, he asks for a small lie: 'Tell me the accusation is false and I will let you go. Is it true that you claim to be a king?'[13]

The difference between the representative of the Roman Empire and that of the Kingdom of Truth is evident at last. The procurator represents an authority which abuses its power. Partisanship and violence are the rules by which he governs. It is the reason of force which wins over the force of reason.

Jesus, on the other hand, embodies the destiny of the martyrs from Able to the present time, victims of their integrity. What other destiny can await a helpless prisoner, facing an absolute power and a crowd which is being manipulated to demand His death, when all He has is the truth on His side?

What is the truth? Pilate understands a little about truth, and cares even less. In his interrogation he tries only to find out how dangerous the prisoner is. Once he is sure that Jesus does not aspire after power, he no longer cares what the prisoner may say.

Jesus is also quiet. If Pilate had been a fisherman, a prostitute, or a tax collector, He would have carried the topic a bit further and said as He had the night before: 'I am the Way and the Truth and the Life.'[14]

But Pilate would not have understood such words. He considers himself too culturally superior to be able to learn something from this prisoner. Besides, as a politician he is more interested in public opinion than in the private views of one man. When Pilate chose not to listen to his prisoner, he was choosing not to listen to the most profound and influential thinker that the Empire would ever know.[15]

Strange paradox of history, that the name of Pontius Pilate would be remembered by posterity only for discrediting a mysterious prisoner on a spring morning in the year AD31

... a prisoner who, without even appearing in the official annals, would become the focus of all history.[16]

If Pilate had acted out of integrity and completed his duty, he would have freed Jesus. But by abusing his authority, he added himself to the infamous list of the hangmen of all time. He joined the rank of opportunists, of the irresponsible and of those whom the Bible defines as monsters. The terrible beasts described in the visions of Daniel and Revelation represent all power which is abusive, all governments which, by opposing justice, become enemies of God, especially when they have the audacity to pretend to act in His name.

Although the governor is undoubtedly a professional, capable of being just, in this paradoxical trial, he never discovers the truth about his defendant, because he does not listen to His answers. If in a given moment he decides to defend the prisoner, it is more out of hatred of the accusers than out of respect for Jesus.

Pilate's question, 'What is truth?' is a fundamental one. Throughout the ages wise men and saints have never ceased to ask the same question. Yet many remain unsatisfied because they do not accept the truth when it is offered to them. The truth can change our lives only when we choose to act upon it. Pilate has chosen to disregard the truth, and his decision will ultimately lead to some disastrous consequences.

In this complicated world where everyone proclaims his own understanding of truth, where it is so easy to be mistaken and tricked, how can we find this sure light, this firm ground where we can rest and upon which we may confidently build our lives?

To find the truth — this 'reality which we cannot rationally deny'[17] — it is necessary to desire it and search for it in all sincerity.

The truth, in common with all precious gems, has various facets. To embrace it we need to see it in its totality. A part of the truth isn't truth. And half-truths become particularly despicable within the spiritual realm where the human experience is at its most profound level.

We all know the old oriental fable of the blind men and the elephant[18] which underlines the common tendency to confuse the truth with only one aspect of it. For the true searcher, faith isn't enough; it must be accompanied by correct information. Truth is not synonymous with sincerity. Sincerity is subjective and therefore very difficult to judge. Truth is objective and susceptible to being judged. Sincerity in truth is always preferable to sincerity in error.

Confusing truth and opinion would not be serious if we were able to admit that we might not know best. The problem lies in the fact that from defending our opinion to defending our stubbornness there is only one step.

It has been said that there is nothing more cherished than our own opinions, and nothing more difficult to abandon.[19] The wise man, Solomon, said that 'one can expect more from the foolish man than from the self-opinionated',[20] and that 'the only wise one is he who listens to counsel.'[21]

Everyone has an inalienable right to a free conscience, to believe what he chooses, or to choose not to believe anything at all. We all have the right to look for truth or to run from it. But this does not mean that all attitudes are equally wise. Although we may not be able to embrace it fully, there is only one Transcendent Truth. For this reason, when our opinions have no measure or criteria except our own judgement, we become very much like those poor blind men of the fable, determined to confuse an elephant with a tree trunk or a piece of rope.

To be authentically sincere means to look for the truth at its sources and by all the means available to us.

However, it is often the case that those who most oppose the sacred Scriptures have only a superficial knowledge of them. It is as if they feared that if they studied more they might discover something they did not like. Their rejection of the Bible gives them a certain perverted sense of security.

Although religion is the privileged place from which man may meet the Supreme Truth, all too often we find many 'truths' in confrontation.

And yet, truth is liberating by its very nature. Jesus said, 'You will know the truth, and the truth will set you free.'[22]

Faithfulness to the truth can be compared to the faithfulness of the needle to the pole. Directing the needle to yourself or to others is dangerous. To be faithful to its job, it must always be allowed to move freely.

If God did not exist then truth (that is, in the moral and religious areas) would be relative. But since He does exist He is our supreme point of reference. Our efforts without Him lead only to human truths, all of which are relative. For this reason, we need to listen not only to nature and our consciences but to the revelation which Jesus came to reveal, this 'True Light which gives light to every man who comes into the world'.[23] He is the Light which allows us to discover and confront reality realistically.

This eternal truth (which has been searched for by all philosophers of all ages) is not a theoretical discovery but an existential one which requires total commitment, which liberates us from our fears and allows us to realize our full potential. Besides convincing us, it transforms us. For this reason, merely knowing it is not enough. We must live it. Living our lives in harmony with the truth leads to possessing it, and finally to being possessed by it.

But Pilate is not concerned with truth. What concerns him most at this moment is his political future. He fears the religious leaders who stand accusing Jesus. He knows that if he commits a tactical error his enemies will report him to Caesar. These fears lead him to compromise and delay. They lead him down the path of injustice, concession by concession.

Now he is left with only two choices. He can give in shamefully after so much resistance or he can confront the dominant class of the land.

He wants to finish with this vexatious case and he wants an acquittal, even if he must resort to physical torture[24] in order to get it. He sends Jesus to be flogged.[25] Without realizing it he has put in motion the violence which will lead inexorably to the final, cruel ending.[26]

Pilate soon discovers that his shameful 'solution' still does not rid him of the prisoner. Disfigured and bleeding,

Jesus stands serenely before Pilate, challenging him to reveal whether he is a just judge or a cowardly cheat.

In one final desperate attempt to save face, Pilate presents Jesus to the crowd: 'Here is the man.'[27]

With these words Pilate invites the whole world to look upon Jesus, the representative of human suffering and of the humiliated. Abandoned by those who claim to be on His side, beaten by the powerful, and manipulated by those who claim to be God's representatives, Jesus truly is the Man of Sorrows spoken of by the prophets.[28] He is the man who has come to take upon Himself the human condition in all its aspects, in order to save mankind from its dehumanization.

But here, for all to see, stands only a prisoner awaiting the death sentence. They cannot imagine the far-reaching effect that His death will have.[29]

No one knew that God was carrying out His plans in spite of the corruption in the legal system, the lying of the clergy and the weakness of Pilate. The cross revealed that in spite of appearances we are not alone in our unjust world. It proved that God, because of His desire to bring us back to life, was capable of sharing our precarious existence, even to the point of facing death. Without placing limits upon human freedom, God's plan of salvation began to triumph when apparently it was being trodden underfoot by those it was meant to save. In a mysterious way which only Divine Grace can understand, the love of the one who willingly spilled His own blood was strong enough to defeat the hatred of the world.

By raising the thirst for justice, Jesus on the cross was beginning to win hearts, including those of His executioners, making them desire the possibility of forgiveness for their sins and of a better life.[30] Time would prove just how right Jesus was when He said that He had come so that the truth could reign.

The crowd stares up at the bleeding prisoner. But His enemies will never be satisfied with so little. One of them shouts out above the noise: 'If you let this man go, you are no friend of Caesar.'[31]

He has found Pilate's weak spot. Pilate's future as a

Roman magistrate depends on Caesar. An accusation of political vacillation presented in the most persuasive way by expert barristers could lead to his downfall.[32]

Perturbed by the pressure being exerted upon him and by his own confused feelings, Pilate asks loudly: 'What shall I do, then, with Jesus, who is called Christ?'[33]

What will Pilate do? Trying to preserve his position, he does what the Pilates of all times have always done. He does what is most convenient for him at the moment.

Our decisions do not always stem from our convictions either. Too often we base our decisions upon circumstances or upon our courage or lack of it. Sometimes we do not even have a clear idea of our true motives when we choose to act or not to act. More often than we care to admit, we, like Pilate, choose to ignore the truth, even when it stands before us wounded and bleeding.

The procurator's last question reveals the depths of his abdication: 'Shall I crucify your king?'

The hierarchy know now that they have won, and wishing to seal Jesus' fate, they cry: 'We have no king but Caesar!'[34]

History would be sure to turn this tactical lie into painful truth.[35] Unwilling to change their minds these men who claim to wait for the Messiah finally reject Him. They have chosen to defend their positions so they condemn themselves to the darkness of error.

Stubbornness and insincerity can blind us, too. Through stubbornness our personal or historical errors convert themselves into prejudices, traditions, and dogmas, chaining us and restricting our freedom. And what is worse, it also restricts the freedom of others. It is too easy to appoint oneself the apostle for truth, proclaiming it to the four winds at the risk of becoming bigoted and intolerant.[36]

Even the Bible can be manipulated and utilized to uphold personal or group agendas. The results stretch from merely picturesque heresies to bloody holy wars. Anyone who puts his mind to it is able to twist not only the difficult passages but also the most clear and simple.[37]

The truth does not need our defence. It can stand alone

against everything. However, it can always benefit from our testimony.

Surrounded by the clamouring crowd which is calling for the prisoner's crucifixion,[38] Pilate gives in. He has tried to get rid of Jesus by confirming His innocence, by sending Him to Herod, by negotiating His release in exchange for Barabbas, by beating Him in order to quench the accusers' thirst for blood and to incite pity. Everything has failed.

The only thing the Governor has refused to do is to put himself at risk in order to save the strange prisoner. He refuses to be put at odds with the government in Rome. Succumbing to the tyranny of 'what will they say', Pilate finishes the business with the theatrical gesture of washing his hands.[39]

But water does not cleanse anybody from the guilt of a crime, and Pilate's hands remain as stained as before. The prisoner's silence will weigh upon him through the coming years as a penalty worse than death. He will try to forget the whole affair, but the calm and quiet look of that dying man will remain with him forever.

The inscription which Pilate orders to be placed on the cross sounds almost like a confession meant to right the wrong done: 'Jesus of Nazareth, King of the Jews.'[40]

Not wanting to complicate his life, Pilate ignored the truth. He scorned and ridiculed it, silenced and negated it, eliminated and buried it. But nobody wins when he sacrifices his ethical values. Resisting the truth always brings disastrous consequences. Pilate will discover soon enough the uselessness of his concessions.

Soon after Jesus' trial Pilate will be accused by the same men who have pushed him to condemn Jesus. He will be deposed. Finally, he will be exiled to Gaul by the Emperor Caligula.[41]

What would have happened to Pilate had he remained faithful to his convictions and released Jesus? Probably nothing. Most likely, time would have demonstrated that the accusations against Jesus were false. Perhaps, in the worst case, Tiberius would have removed him from office. But Pilate would have taken with him his own peace of mind.

Pilate's wife is truer to herself. Her own personal knowledge of Jesus and a strange dream which tormented her the night before persuade her that Jesus is innocent. In vain she fearfully warns her husband: 'Do not have anything to do with that innocent man, for I have suffered a great deal today in a dream because of him.'[42]

An old legend says that in her dream Procula was told that from age to age and in all the languages it would be said that Jesus died under Pontius Pilate.[43]

According to tradition, the shadow of a cross would haunt Pilate's memory and, until his death, he would be tortured by the incurable obsession of washing from his hands those indelible bloodstains.[44]

Yet the trial of Jesus continues to this day. His testimony for the truth still shines down on us. Today, as on that day long ago, those who do not wish to commit themselves continue to prefer the backing of power and the majority.

Each time we silence our consciences by saying that it is better to avoid conflicts and that we must know when to wait and when to negotiate, we are acting like Pilate. Each time we call weakness wisdom and cowardice patience, we inflict the wounds all over again.

Because it is risky, the truth which is drunk from the fountains is always minimal and only the valiant dare to drink of it. Since the truth is independent of its supporters, since it is not decided by vote nor imposed by law, since it is not adopted by popular acclaim, it does not tend to be supported by the masses or their leaders. It does have Christ, however. As happened to Him, His followers are often treated as crazy, occasionally as heroes, often as martyrs, and always as dissidents.

'The Gospel of John sets this event in a place call in Greek 'Lithostrotos' and in Hebrew 'Gabbatha', which means, 'the place of tiled pavement' (19:13), which has been located in the great patio of the Tower Antonia (Pierre Benoit, 'L'Antonia d'Herode le Grand et le Forum oriental d'Aelia capitolma', Harvard Theological Review, vol. 64, 1971). To administer justice, the Roman Magistrate worked in the 'praetorium' which was made up of two sections: the 'tribunal' (a semicircular platform, easy to transport and set up wherever it seemed convenient), and the judgement seat which was placed on the platform and where the judge sat to administer sentences. The proceedings followed by Pilate were usual in those cases. (cf. Cicero, *Pro Cluentio* 58.)

²The description of Jesus' trial before Pilate is given in Matt. 27:1-31; Mark 15:1-21; Luke 23:1-25 and John 18:28 to 19:16.

³John 18:33. Without doubt Pilate would have released Jesus if he had regarded Him as crazy. In the year 62, the acting procurator refused to condemn another Jesus, son of Ananias, also accused of prophesying to destroy the Temple (Josephus, *War* 6:300-309; cf. Mark 14:55-59).

⁴John 18:33-35; cf. Matt. 27:11-14.

⁵The Romans had given the Sanhedrin power to try cases and pronounce sentence according to Jewish legislation. However, Augustus had limited its power. All death sentences had to be ratified by the Roman authorities. Consequently, the ius gladii pertained exclusively to the proconsul. The biblical text makes this very clear (John 18:31). If the Sanhedrin consulted with the Roman official it wasn't to fix a fine or for excommunication, or for the thirty-nine whiplashes which were mandatory for certain crimes (2 Cor. 11:24), since they could authorize all of those without Roman authorization. What they wanted was permission to execute capital punishment.

⁶Luke 22:24-30.

⁷See specifically Matt. 23:1-36. The political implications of Jesus' action explain in part the hostility of the leaders of the country (cf. John 11:45-53).

⁸Matt. 5:21-26, 38-48.

⁹John 18:36, 37.

¹⁰John 18:38.

¹¹Giovanni Papini, *Historia de Cristo*, Porrua, Mexico DF, 1984, page 186.

¹²Luis Bonnet and Alberto Schroeder, *Comentario del Nuevo Testamento*, Casa Bautista de Publicaciones, 1970, t.2, page 338.

¹³John 18:37.

¹⁴John 14:6.

¹⁵On this point see Juan Mateos and Juan Barreto, *El Evangelio de Juan*, Cristiandad, Madrid, 1982, page 778.

¹⁶Aside from his encounter with Jesus, history tells us only that Pontius Pilate was the Roman representative and served as prefect of Judea under Tiberius in the years AD26 to 36, when he was relieved of his duties because of his poor performance as a politician, and was returned to Rome. The only archaeological testimony that Pilate governed Palestine is a fragmentary inscription in stone, found at Caesarea in 1961.

¹⁷Plato, *Leges* 663.

¹⁸An old oriental fable says that in a far-away town a traveller arrived one day riding an elephant. Upon finding out about the event, some blind men who begged by the side of the road asked if they might touch it for a moment in order to have an idea of what an elephant was like. They then began to touch the beast. When the visitor continued on his journey, the blind began to argue among themselves about what they had touched with their hands. One had touched the belly of the elephant and he defined it as a huge

wrinkled ball. Another had touched the leg and described the elephant as a tree trunk; the one who had touched the trunk compared it to a soft snake; and the last, who had managed to touch only the tail, described the great animal as a small cord. And so they could not agree and parted enemies, when, if they had only stopped to put together all that they knew, they would have had a true idea of what an elephant was like.

[19]'The sin that is most nearly hopeless and incurable is pride of opinion or self-conceit.' (Ellen G. White, *Testimonies for the church*, Pacific Press, Mountain View (California), 1948, vol. 7, pages 199, 200.)

[20]Prov. 26:12.

[21]Prov. 12:15; Rom. 12:16.

[22]John 8:32.

[23]John 1:9.

[24]This was without doubt the motive which caused him, upon finding out that Jesus came from Galilee, to send Him to Herod, tetrarch of that region and who was in Jerusalem because of the Passover holidays (Luke 23:5-12). In Roman law, the power of the court was determined by either the place of detention (forum aprehensionis) or the place where the crime had been committed (forum originis). Herod, therefore, did not have jurisdiction in this case since Jesus had been detained in Judea for the crime of 'political agitation' which affected the entire country and not just Galilee. Pilate took advantage of Herod's presence to avoid declaring judgement, thus obtaining a supporting decree of innocence. About the jurisdictional irregularities of the trial of Jesus, see Paul Winter, *On the Trial of Jesus*, Berlin: Studia Judaica, 1974.

[25]John 19:1-4.

[26]Philo of Alexandria, Pilate's contemporary, describes him as someone 'of boisterous personality, obsessive and cruel', (*Embassy to Gaius* 38).

[27]John 19:5; cf. Ellen G. White, *The Desire of Ages*, page 735.

[28]Isa. 52:13 to 53:12.

[29]All the eyewitness accounts of the crucifixion and burial of Jesus culminate in the story of the resurrection: Matt. 28:1-15; Mark 16:1-18; Luke 24:1-49; John 20:1-29; 21:1-19.

[30]The salvation consequences of the sacrifice at Calvary constitute what the Bible calls 'the mystery of grace'. (1 Tim. 3:16), explained in the epistles (Eph. 2:1-22; Rom. 3:21-26; 5:1-11; 2 Cor. 5:11 to 6:2, etc.). The importance and complexity of the theme doesn't allow us to tackle it here.

[31]John 19:12.

[32]The numerous grievances committed by Pilate against the people had made him absolutely unpopular. One of his first mistakes was to transfer the military quarters from Caesarea to Jerusalem, where the presence of military standards represented idolatrous images to the strict Jews. This excited such indignation that they tumultuously broke into the procurator's residence to force him to remove the offensive images from the Holy City immediately. Irritated by the uprising, Pilate ordered his soldiers to surround them and kill all who did not leave. When they demonstrated that they preferred to die before permitting the Holy City to be profaned, he had to back down. His reign

was full of cruel acts, such as the massacre of Galilean pilgrims, narrated in Luke 13:1-3, (cf. Josephus, *War* 2:169). His treatment of Jesus reflects his insecure frame of mind.

[33] Matt. 27:22.

[34] John 19:15.

[35] Josephus describes in total detail the circumstances which launched Israel into the war against the Romans in the years AD66 to 70 (*War* 2:284 to 7:20). The city of Jerusalem and the Temple were taken by Titus and flattened in AD70-71. Of all the buildings in the city, only three towers and part of the west wall remained standing. In the year 135 the emperor Adriano established a Roman colony there. To erase all strands of Judaism, he changed the name of the city to Aelia Capitolina, and dedicated the location of the Temple to Jupiter (Eusebius, *Historia ecclesiastica IV*, 6:1-4). The Jews were exiled, under penalty of death, and Israel as a political entity ceased to exist in Palestine until 1948.

[36] For this idea see Voltaire, *Lettre a D'Alembert*, February 1776.

[37] Ellen G. White, *The Great Controversy*, Mountain View (California), Pacific Press, 1977, pages 656-658; *Selected Messages*, t. 1, pages 49, 50.

[38] Matt. 27:22; Mark 15:14; Luke 23:20-23; John 19:6, 14-16. The punishment of the crucifixion was commonly practised by the Romans in the first century of our era. Ciceron calls it 'the cruellest and most shameful torture'; 'that a Roman citizen be bound is an abuse; that he be beaten is a crime; that he be executed is almost parricide. What can I say, then, if he is hung from a cross? For something so abominable there is no adequate word for it.' (*De finibis* 5:92.) Philo states that 'it was the lowest and meanest way that an evil life can be terminated'. (*De providentia* 2:24, 25.) Josephus describes numerous crucifixions, some massive ones, throughout the conflict between Israel and Rome (*War* 5:44 to 51; 2:75, 253, 306, 308; 3:321; 5:289; *Ant.* 17:295; 2:241; 20:119; etc.). Normally it was applied only to seditious slaves or to cases of high treason. The condemned was hanged as an example at the entrance to the city or by the side of the road. They hung an inscription which indicated the crime committed, either around the prisoner's neck or above him on the cross. Although there were crosses of various types, the Romans tended to hang prisoners from a crossbar which was called 'patibulum' which was placed at the top of the post (cruxcommissa) or lower in a groove (crux immisa). The condemned was nailed or tied by the hands and feet and hung naked (by right the clothing belonged to the executioner) in the double torment of torture and shame. To the Jews crucifixion was proof of Divine punishment (Deut. 21:22, 23; Gal. 3:13). Death in this way, which could be slow coming, generally resulted from asphyxia, because of exhaustion, respiratory and circulatory difficulties. The agony could be cut by breaking the prisoner's legs which prevented him from pushing himself up to breathe (see Martin Hengel, *Crucifixion*, Fortress Press, Philadelphia, 1977). In June 1968 the remains of a twenty-five-year-old named John, son of Haggai, were found in the cemetery Giv'at ha Mivtar, north of Jerusalem in niche no. 9 along with other remains from the first century. The bones of the heel had been pierced by a nail 18 centimetres long which held them together and

which were pulled from the cross along with a piece of olive wood. The tibia bones were broken by various blows and the wrists had been nailed. This is the archaeological finding which appears the most similar to the crucifixion described by the gospels (Jacques Briend, *Bible et Terre Sainte*, July-August 1971, page 8).

[39] Matt. 27:24.

[40] Matt. 27:37; Mark 15:26; Luke 23:38; John 19:19.

[41] Late historical facts, difficult to verify, say that Pilate was exiled by Caligula to Vienne, a Gaulish city halfway between the actual French city of Valence and the Swiss city of Geneva, and that there he committed suicide. A much less viable story links his name, his regrets and his suicide to Mt. Pilate, to the south of Lake Lucerne in Switzerland.

[42] Matt. 27:19.

[43] Dorothy L. Sayers, *The Man Born to be King*, cited by Karl Barth, Esquisse d'une dogmatique, Neuchatel/Paris, Delachaux and Niestle, 1968, pages 173-181.

[44] An apocryphal writing called 'Letter of Pilate to Claudius' known by Tertulian before AD197 along with 'Correspondence with Tiberius' from the Middle Ages is attributed to him.

In the evening

The feast has ended on a bitter note. Sunday evening is drawing on.¹ Tired and discouraged, two travellers make their way home. Cleopas and his companion² cannot forget the brutal death of their beloved Master on the previous Friday afternoon. His last words, His arrest, the death decree, the torture, and His end on the cross haunt them³ as they make their way along the road to Emmaus.⁴

More painful than the indignation over the death of an innocent person or the sorrow over the loss of a dear friend, and greater than the fear that they, too, might end up being prosecuted, is the shattering blow of having lost their faith and their hope. Everything that had given their lives meaning lay buried in the borrowed tomb outside Jerusalem.⁵

Even more disconcerting than the life of the Nazarene had been His death. If His teachings had broken all their plans, the crucifixion had certainly broken their spirits.

The fact that the man sent by God was humble, gentle with the children and women, friend of the poor and forgiving towards His enemies was hardly acceptable. The fact that the Liberator of Israel had not been capable of liberating Himself, that the Saviour had not done anything to save Himself, was unexplainable.⁶ The fact that the promised Messiah could be assassinated in the gallows of the most abject criminals, that the King who was expected to release His people from the enemy yoke had been executed by the Romans⁷ was too much of a scandal to be credible. If God existed and if Israel mattered to Him, then it was impossible to believe that He had permitted such cruelty to Jesus of Nazareth.

Just when it seems that they have reached the depths of their despair, a third man appears on the road. This stranger does not seem altogether unknown, yet they cannot remember where they have seen him before. The traveller gains their confidence and in the most natural way he asks: '"What are you discussing together as you walk along?"'⁸

128 IN THE EVENING

'"Are you the only one living in Jerusalem who doesn't know the things that have happened in these days?"'[9]

These anguished travellers have much to tell. The stranger listens closely to their story. He seems to understand their profound suffering because he says nothing.

The men tell him, in fragments, of their pain and their disenchantment. They talk of Jesus, their beloved Master, '"a prophet, powerful in word and deed before God and all the people".'[10] They tell how the priests turned Him over to be condemned to death, how the Romans crucified Him, and how He was buried in a borrowed tomb. They relate the disappearance of the body and the incredible hypothesis of a miracle.

'"Some of our women amazed us. They went to the tomb early this morning but didn't find his body. They came and told us that they had seen a vision of angels, who said he was alive. Then some of our companions went to the tomb and found it just as the women had said, but him they did not see."'[11]

From the painful description of the events, they move to an even more painful, personal confession.

'"But we had been hoping that he was the man to liberate Israel."'[12]

The stranger has been waiting for this moment. The travellers have reached the end of the story. They have told everything. Now, shipwrecked by their own helplessness, they can do no more than listen to the stranger. After the bad news of death and injustice, the moment has come for the latest news . . . news of life and of hope.

When the weary men finally admit their despair, the stranger begins to reveal the true reality to which they are blind. He transforms old prophecies into new promises. Through His words, familiar and yet so new, the events of the weekend begin to carry unexpected perspectives. The awful crime becomes more than an act of violence; the victim more than a defeated man. In the light of Divine plans the tragedy, the scandal, the cross, and the empty tomb take on a new perspective. In the light of the prophecies they finally recognize that Jesus of Nazareth is the longed-for Liberator.

'Wasn't it written that the Messiah would have to suffer all this in order to enter into His glory?'[13]

Deep within their souls they feel their faith returning like an overflowing spring, pushing hope upwards in great bubbling torrents.

Suddenly they realize that their Jesus, who had been misunderstood, rejected and crucified by His own, had been announced in the Scriptures. By living out the terrible experience of the suffering servant predicted in the prophets, He has in some mysterious way redeemed mankind.[14]

Filled with new hope, yet fearing once more to find themselves alone in the darkness of their doubts, they invite the stranger to stay with them.[15]

He accepts their invitation as if He has been awaiting it, and enters their house to share in their hospitality. He has comforted their afflicted souls. Now the time has come to feed their hungry bodies. He takes the bread, blesses it and breaks it.

In that instant the disciples discover, in astonishment, that their strange guest is none other than Jesus.[16] They had not been able to recognize Him by His features, by the light in His eyes, nor by the tone of His voice. But those hands marked by human evil and opened in that familiar gesture of acceptance are enough.

'Were not our hearts burning within us while he talked with us on the road and opened the Scriptures to us? How were we unable to see him before?'[17]

We understand their sorrow for we, too, have walked the road of doubt. We have all walked the painful path which leads us into the fog of discouragement. We know the anguish of walking in the dark, lost and without help. We have all suffered, at some time, the absence of God. We have all cried out in the night, 'Where are you, God? Why don't you answer me?'

For many, the silence of God is an excuse not to believe. For others it serves as an excuse to trust only in themselves. It permits them to hypothesize that a Supreme Being really doesn't exist.

But for the one who wants to believe, the silence of God is the hardest test that his faith must endure:

'Why doesn't God listen to me? Why doesn't He answer me? What have I done?'

Job debated in the middle of this agony which we all experience until he discovered that man's reproach towards God's silence is really his reproach to God for not responding to him in the way he desires.[18] It is the desire that He put Himself at man's disposal rather than man's putting himself at His. In other words, he wants a God in his image and likeness.

Our trauma is caused by our rejection of a God who lets man be man, and who, like God, cannot stop being God. We suffer because we do not want to understand that although He is always on the lookout for us, and although He talks to us in 'many times and in many ways',[19] it is usually in a secret way.

We often feel, like the travellers in our story, that God seems to abandon us at the time when we need Him most. The overwhelming injustice and misery in our world makes us cry out as did Jesus: '"My God, my God, why have you forsaken me?"'[20]

No matter how strong we may feel, we all eventually must admit our helplessness in the face of the terrible suffering which is brought on by injustice and evil. It is at these times when we feel so alone. Finally, when we admit that we need more courage than we are able to summon from within in order to believe, we allow God to reveal Himself to us again.

Sometimes we fail to see Jesus. We allow our problems to cloud our vision. We lament the absence of God. Our eyes are blinded in spite of all the indications of His presence. Not even in the most inspiring worship service nor in our most intimate prayers can we perceive His presence by our side.

Like the disciples of Emmaus, we need to learn to listen and to look beyond the veil of divine silence and that of human deafness and blindness to the revelations of the Eternal Presence. It is not for us to question God's love and absolute wisdom, based upon our faulty perceptions of His interventions or absences in our own particular lives.

If God does not seem to be responding immediately and magically in the way we want, it is because He respects our freedom. Rather than imposing Himself through high profile interventions, God often prefers working silently through us. In this way He allows us to discover for ourselves the joy of giving and loving.

It is crucial that we discover His presence, but we must also accept His absence. Once we have discovered that He is always present, He leaves us with the assurance of His spiritual assistance. He is no longer merely Someone important in our lives. He is the reason for our existence.[21]

With renewed energy, Cleopas and his friend run back to the city. Now distance does not matter. There are no obstacles or fears. Only one thing is important. They must tell everyone, beginning with their friends, that Jesus, whom they all believed to be dead, has been resurrected and now lives forever.[22]

Their story reaches beyond Jerusalem. It reaches us as well. It assures us that although we are suffering and doubting, lost in the night of our struggles, we are not alone. Someone is there in the silence accompanying us, no matter how twisted our paths are, towards our personal Emmaus.

---

[1] Text based on Luke 24:13-35 (cf. Mark 16:12, 13).

[2] Cleopas is perhaps the semitic equivalent to the Greek 'Kleopatros'. We know the husband of Mary, mother of James the younger and Joseph and one of the women who watched the crucifixion, by this name. (John 19:25; cf. Matt. 27:55, 56; Mark 15:40.) The anonymity of his companion on the journey has sparked various hypotheses, among which is that it could have been his own wife who returned home with him (K. Bornhauser, *The Death and Resurrection of Jesus Christ*, Bangalore, London, 1958, pages 221, 222). The ancient church identifies this Cleopas with a brother of Joseph, Jesus' adoptive father (Eusebius, *Historia eclesiastica III*: 11, 32; IV: 22).

[3] About the account of Jesus' crucifixion, see Matt. 27:1-56; Mark 15:1-41; Luke 23:1-49; John 19:1-37.

[4] The location of this town presents some problems: 'Amwas' is fifteen miles (that is 160 furlongs as some manuscripts indicate). Josephus mentions a military colony with the name of Ammaus established by Vespasian at 30 furlongs to the west of Jerusalem (*War* 7:217). Today the supposed place

of Emmaus is called 'el-Qubeibe'. If Emmaus was 60 furlongs from Jerusalem (Luke 24:13) and we consider that the furlong is 660 feet (220 yards), the distance was approximately seven and a half miles.

[5] Regarding the sepulchre of Jesus, see Matt. 27:57-61; Mark 15:42-47; Luke 23:50-56 and John 19:38-42.

[6] Jesus, on the cross, had prayed for His executioners, saying: 'Father, forgive them, for they know not what they do.' (Luke 23:34.)

[7] It should not be forgotten that officially Jesus was judged as being more deserving of death than Barabbas, a seditious and murderous criminal (Luke 23:13-25), and was crucified between two malefactors (Luke 23:32), thieves (Matt. 27:38), also called hold-up men or bandits (Mark 15:27).

[8] Luke 24:15-17 (NIV).
[9] Luke 24:18 (NIV).
[10] Luke 24:19, 20 (NIV).
[11] Luke 24:22-24 (NIV).
[12] Luke 24:21 (NEB).
[13] Luke 24:25-27; cf. 44-48.

[14] Among the texts of Moses to which Jesus refers are perhaps Gen. 3:15; 22:18; Num. 21:9; Deut. 8:15, 18, 19; and among those of the prophets, perhaps Isa. 40:10, 11; 50:4-7; 52:13 to 53:12; 61:1-3; 63:1-6; Jer. 33:14-16; Dan. 9:24-27; Mic. 5:2; Zech. 9:9; 12:10.

[15] Luke 24:28, 29.
[16] Luke 24:30, 31.
[17] Luke 24:32.
[18] Job 42:1-6.
[19] Heb. 1:1-3.

[20] Matt. 27:46 (NIV); Mark 15:34 (citing Ps. 22:1). Regarding Jesus' feelings of aloneness and abandonment on the cross, see *The Desire of Ages*, pages 741-757.

[21] See how Paul formulates this experience: Gal. 2:20; Phil. 1:21; 4:13; Col. 1:27; 3:3, 4.

[22] Luke 24:33-35, cf. *The Desire of Ages*, page 795.

Among friends

The news travels fast. It is an incredible story. They know it is true, not because they wish it were so as those who do not believe pretend, but because anyone who has really known Him knows that it has to be this way. Jesus is not a figment of their imagination. He is the most splendid person who has ever existed. He has risen and now lives forever.[1]

This is why they gather together here tonight,[2] waiting expectantly in this special upper room.[3] They meet together, despite the persecution ordered by those who hope that their faith is unfounded.[4]

Soon after, country folk and fishermen see Jesus, together with artisans, housewives, government employees, and doctors. Soldiers, common labourers, beggars, and foreigners. Poor and rich, men and women, old and young, more than 500 strong, see the risen Jesus — this time in an outdoor location in Galilee.[5]

Joseph of Arimathea is here[6] with other aristocrats, priests and pharisees[7] who have been expelled from the Sanhedrin and excommunicated[8] for embracing this new sect.[9] They have decided to use their influence and talents for their Master.

There is a Roman centurion here,[10] along with some soldiers who have given up their arms in order to enlist in the fight for peace.

Simon is here along with other terrorists who have escaped from prison and managed to outlive their crimes. They fight now with more courage than ever, not for their nationalistic pride but for a freedom without borders or classes and one that is more all-embracing than all the civil liberties combined.

Matthew, ex-tax-collector, is also here with his fellow bankers. They are no longer interested in enriching themselves but in sharing their wealth with more needy folk and trying to convince their old clients that the soundest investment is in the treasury of heaven, where profit is guaranteed forever.[11]

Mary Magdalene[12] and other famous ex-prostitutes are here as well. They are free now and living for an eternal love.

There are even some Essenes here,[13] evicted from their monastery for comprehending that God prefers man to live in brotherhood, not in isolation.

They are so different yet they are united. They have each experienced the great encounter of their lives.

Jesus had seen, beneath the gaudy makeup of the prostitute, a desire for help. He had seen, behind the stubborn arguments of a doctor of the law, a deep insecurity and a true desire to find the truth. In the trembling of one man perched in a tree, He had seen the spiritual thirst of a marginated man who could no longer stand the loneliness. In the irritating complaints of Martha, He heard her cry for acceptance and saw her need to find a coherent scale of values. Jesus discovered, behind the intellectual curiosity of an elegant young man, the anguish of a dissatisfied soul, vacillating between his own selfish interests and his thirst for the ideal.

What would have become of each of these if they had not been found by Jesus? What would have happened to Mary? Would she have died, stoned by the respectable townsfolk? Or would she have continued putting up with life in the brothel until she was consumed by the misery of being forgotten or by some fatal illness?

What would have become of the Gerasene and of the other demon-possessed folk if they had not been rescued by Jesus? How long would the exorcists have been allowed to torment them before they were finally hunted and burnt as wizards?

What would have become of the faith and sanity of a deaf-and-dumb boy's father if Jesus had not helped him to believe?

What would have become of Nicodemus and the other theologians if they had not found in that night meeting the true meaning of religion?

What would have become of the rest — of John, of Andrew, of Cleopas and his friend, if they had not encountered in Jesus the meaning of their existence?

What would have happened to each of us if Jesus had not come to restore peace to our fast-paced life? What would we have believed in if Jesus had not shown Himself to us? What would we have substituted in our search for meaning?

No one knows how Jesus enters the room.[14] All they know is that He has come. They are not surprised for Jesus has proven His love for them in so many ways before.

Jesus stands among them, and the room suddenly goes quiet. Everyone waits to hear what He has come to say. Jesus looks about, and with that characteristic smile stretching across His tanned face and lighting up His eyes He greets them, one by one.

Finally, He addresses them as a group. His voice is filled with love and pride: 'I have fulfilled everything that was written in the law and the prophets. I suffered and died for each of you and I rose again on the third day so that you could receive forgiveness from above. You are my witnesses to this.'

He pauses a moment as if dreading the goodbye which must come. Finally, He makes His last great announcement: 'I must now go to my Father. But I will send the Holy Spirit. He will comfort you and teach you. He will remain with you until I return.'

It seems a sad announcement. But Jesus knows that it is the best way. Instead of inviting His followers to look back, making them taxpayers to a past which will seem further and further away with each passing day, He prefers that they examine the horizon and that they wait for the day of His return with growing anticipation.

It is nearly time for Him to go, but Jesus still has one important thing to tell them. Raising His hands in blessing, He charges them: 'I have revealed myself to you. Now it is time for you to go and tell others about me. You must go to all the nations and make disciples. I need each of you to go out and befriend others, to love them for me as I have loved you.'[15]

Jesus knows that some will face scorn. Others will face persecution. Wishing to give them strength, He spreads His arms as if to embrace them all: 'I will be with you always, to the end of the age.'

He is gone. Filled with joy and urgency, Jesus' friends hurry to spread the news to the four winds. Some will use their voices, others their pens, and still others will use their lifeblood. Those men and women, who were no more believable or gifted than we are, were able to ignore all the risks and share Jesus, compelled by the certainty that He would fulfil His promise and return again.[16]

Jesus entrusts His story and His reputation to us as well. Humanity tends to set up classes, categories, hierarchies and lists. Jesus asked only for friends. He did not set up an institution or a system to finish His work. All too often we prefer to depend upon a board, a professional group or a ministerial body. But Jesus prefers the personal testimony of each of His followers. He asks us to share with others what we have learned from our own experience with Him.

Jesus prefers it because He knows that without our personal touch, the encounters of the gospels would become no more than interesting literature. He wants us to reimplant with each telling the voice, the heart, and the breath.

For, in fact, the last page of the Gospel remains unwritten, waiting for the story of our personal meeting with Him.

---

[1] For more about the stories of the resurrection, see Matt. 28:1-15; Mark 16:1-15; Luke 24:1-12; John 20:1-18.

[2] Text based on Luke 24:33-53 and John 20:19-31.

[3] Acts 1:3, 4, 13, 14.

[4] John 20:19; Matt. 28:11-15; cf. Acts 4:1-31; 5:17-42.

[5] 1 Cor. 15:6.

[6] Matt. 27:57-61; Mark 15:42-47; Luke 23:50-56; John 19:38-42.

[7] John 19:39 cites Nicodemus, one of the 'greatest' of the Jews (John 3:1). Acts 6:7 speaks of many priests converted to Christianity, and Acts 15:5 speaks of Pharisees who were members of the young church.

[8] John 9:22, 34, 35 testifies to the fact that the menace of being excommunicated for being a Christian existed even during Jesus' life.

[9] The first name given to Jesus' followers was 'the way' (Acts 19:9, 23; 16:17; 18:25, 26; 22:4), and they were considered early on as a sect (Acts 24:5; 28:22). Jesus' followers began to be called Christians for the first time in Antioch (Acts 11:26), perhaps even before the persecution ordered by Herod Agrippa (AD41-44; Acts 12:1-3).

[10] Hypothesis based on Matt. 27:54; Mark 15:39 and Luke 23:47.

[11] See Matt. 6:19-21.

[12] The testimony of the gospels is unanimous in the recognition that Mary Magdalene was the first witness of the resurrection: Mark 16:9-11; cf. 1-8, 12-14; John 20:11-18; Matt. 28:1-10.

[13] Beside the monastery at Qumran, the largest community of Essenes that we know about was in Damascus. In 1897 a book was discovered in Cairo called *The document of Damascus* (or the Zadokite Document, published in 1910) which describes them as 'the community of the new covenant' which must have been established in Damascus; and which had much in common with the 'Rule of the Community' of the Qumran. An important conversion to Christianity among the Essenes would explain Saul's persecution of Christians in this city (Acts 9:1-27; 22:1-16; 26:12-20).

[14] See Luke 24:36-49; cf. John 20:19-23; 1 Cor. 15:6. The place could be the upper room of the Last Supper (Luke 22:12-23) and of the pouring out of the Holy Spirit at Pentecost (Acts 1:12 and 2:5). The sightings of the resurrected Jesus were numerous, and He gave 'many signs' of His resurrection to His disciples 'during forty days'.

[15] See Matt. 28:16-20; Mark 16:14-18; Luke 24:44-49; John 20:21-23; cf. Acts 1:1-8. In the Greek text of Matthew the different aspects of Jesus' order — that is: 'to go, to make disciples, to baptize and to teach' — do not serve the same function in the phrase. All are subordinate to 'making disciples'. In the end Jesus gives only one command: 'Make disciples of all the nations', and then explains how this is to be accomplished: by going, by teaching, and by baptizing.

[16] John 14:1-3; Rev. 22:20.